God's Heai

Book Two
Volume One

The Lock & Load Prophecies of God

"God has given this command concerning the evil one ... 'I am digging your grave, and I will bury you, for you are vile.'"
—Nahum 1:14 CT

James M. Massa

Copyright © 2016 James Mark Massa

The Lock & Load Prophecies of God

Printed in the USA

ISBN (print) : 978-1-5375789-4-1

All Rights Reserved. This book is protected by the copyright laws of the United States of America. This book may not be copied or reprinted for commercial gain or profit. The use of short quotations is permitted. Permission will be granted upon request. The author guarantees all contents are original and do not infringe upon the legal rights of any other person or work.

Prepared for Publication By

Palm Tree Publications is a Division of Palm Tree Productions
www.palmtreeproductions.com
PO BOX 122 | KELLER, TX | 76244

There are more than 60 different translations of scripture used in this work. A complete listing of all translations used is located in Appendix C. Abbreviations follow each reference to give proper credit for each version(s) of the Bible used.

TO CONTACT THE AUTHOR:

Sons of the Branch Ministries
P.O. Box 9871 | Bowling Green, KY 42101
270-777-8377 | sonsofthebranch@yahoo.com

www.SonsoftheBranch.com

DEDICATION

This book is dedicated to my brother

DAVID MICHAEL MASSA

His friendly and persistent exhortation made this work possible.

My brother's name reflects his life:

- A man with God's kingly authority (David),
- Leading the way in warfare worship (Michael),
- Singing God's War Songs (Massa) until every demonic enemy is put under the feet of Jesus.

Michael, you are an example and encouragement to me.

CONTENTS

vii	Explanation: Use of Resources in This Book
ix	Author's Note: The Purpose of Prophecy
xvii	Why Read This Book
1	Introduction
13	**VOLUME 1** **WHAT ARE THE LOCK AND LOAD PROPHECIES?**
15	*Chapter 1* Lock And Load Prophecies Release the Roar of the Lord
29	*Chapter 2* God's Progression of Victory in the Four Major Prophets
41	*Chapter 3* Isaiah: Sing God's *Taunting War Songs*
53	*Chapter 4* Jeremiah: Wail God's *Sarcastic Lamentations*
69	*Chapter 5* Ezekiel: Chant God's *Mocking Dirges*
87	*Chapter 6* Daniel: Build God's *Everlasting Kingdom*
103	*Chapter 7* Our Four-Pronged Attack
121	*Conclusion* Destroy Strongholds and Disciple Nations
127	*Appendix A* List of the Lock & Load Prophecies of God
135	*Appendix B* List of the Prophecies Addressing Each Nation and Its Spiritual Stronghold
	Appendix C List of Abbreviations of the Bible Translations
	Meet The Author James Mark Massa

EXPLANATION

USE OF RESOURCES IN THIS BOOK

This Bible study on *The Lock and Load Prophecies of God* utilizes what I call, *The Combined Translations Bible* (CTB, work in progress) technique. When I quote a verse from the Bible, I combine words or phrases from different Bible translations of that verse.

Here is an example from the book of Acts:

> "Repent ye therefore, and be converted, that your sins may be blotted out, and completely taken away when the seasons of refreshing shall come, times of revival and recovery come from the presence of the Lord; that He may send Jesus Christ, which before we preached unto you: **Yet He must remain in heaven, heaven must retain Him until the times of restitution and universal reformation of all things, the great Restoration** which God has spoken by the mouth of **all** His holy prophets since the world began."
>
> Acts 3:19-21 KJV/ASV/CBW/AAT/BBE/RSV/Mof

In this verse I have combined words and phrases from seven translations to bring out the truth in God's Word in a more powerful way (Note: all words in bold print throughout the book are my emphasis). I may repeat a line two or three times to fully reveal what the Spirit of God is saying. Like the verse telling us Jesus *must remain in heaven, heaven must retain Him, until the great Restoration of all things* prophesied by all the prophets since the world began.

The *Combined Translations Bible* compares over 150 different English translations of the Bible (See Appendix C for a list of the Bible translations used for this book).

I also need to mention my "go to" resource I constantly rely upon to discover the meanings of the Hebrew words in the Old Testament. It is the *Hebrew Word Pictures* by Dr. Frank T. Seekins. He takes the original words of the Hebrew language which were in the form of drawings, or pictures (called pictographs) and gives the literal (letter-by-letter) definition of the Hebrew word. His work is full of revelation, and I highly encourage the reader to purchase a copy for their library.

AUTHOR'S NOTE

The Purpose of Prophecy

This is the second book of seven in the *God's Heart of War Series* and will be presented in two volumes. God's arsenal contains spiritual weapons for spiritual warfare—all made available to us in His Word. His weapons are essential for us to gain the victory in the battle raging around us.

I am a retired military officer with thirty years of experience in the armed forces. I served six years in the Marine Corps during the Vietnam War (1970 – 1976), and after a 12 year hiatus, I re-enlisted and served twenty-four more years in the Air Force National Guard during the first Gulf War and the War on Terror (1989 – 2012). As a result, I cannot help but look at the Word of God with the eyes of a soldier.

Everywhere I look in the Bible, all I see is the heart of God as He searches the world looking for men and women to enlist in His Army. He's calling them to come forth, be trained for battle, and bring His victory on earth in these last days.

Whether you agree that a battle is raging or not, doesn't matter: it's still true. We are engaged in spiritual warfare. Why else does Jesus command us to be overcomers? Why does He call His Church to overcome and *"hate the deeds of the Nicolaitanes"* (Rev. 2:6), *"the blasphemy of them…of the synagogue of satan"* (2:9), *"that woman Jezebel"* (2:20), and *"the depths of satan"* (2:24) to name just a few? There is a war going on. He means for us to win it!

> *If there is no battle, nothing to overcome, then why does Jesus call us to be overcomers?*

We will never triumph until we understand and use the specific spiritual weapons the Lord has given us. The path to complete victory in every area of our life is only available if we use the divine weapons God has designated to defeat that specific attack of the evil one. It is just like the natural realm. A soldier does not take out a tank with a rifle; he must use an RPG (rocket propelled grenade) launcher. We must use the weapon that is designed to repel that attack.

It is the same for us in the spiritual realm. We must use the exact spiritual weapon God has provided for us to repel the specific spiritual assault coming against us. Using the Lord's designated Word Weapon along with the anointing of the Holy Spirit, the authority of the blood and name of Jesus, and in the power of His resurrection, God causes us to always triumph.

Our battleground is unique. We're called to engage in warfare worship as we do battle for the heart and soul of God's children. Paul exclaims, *"But praise be to God, Who always causes us to triumph,* **makes us strong to overcome,**

*[He] grants us **complete success** as we sing songs of victory"* (2 Cor. 2:14 CTB/BBE). It's not a partial success but total victory in Jesus.

> We do battle for the heart and soul of God's children in warfare-worship

The Greek word for the phrase *"causes us to triumph"* is the word *thriambeuo* which refers to the songs that are sung after a victory.[1] We are victorious and overcome all the power of the devil, as we sing Jesus' songs of triumph. This word *thriambeuo* is used one other time in the New Testament where Paul tells the Church in Colossae about Jesus' victory on the Cross. Paul says, *"[Jesus has] defeated and stripped the rulers and powers of the spiritual world of their sham authority. With the Cross He won the victory over them, and **showed the world that they were powerless;** He publicly shamed them, like a triumphant general displaying His captives in a victory parade **as He celebrated singing His victory songs**"* (Col. 2:15 ERV/EXB/MSG/TCNT/CTB). We have complete success in Jesus, not only in our own lives but in the lives of our family, city, and nation. Jesus came to bring His victory to the entire world. Yes, we have a very good reason to sing!

Jesus is both Lord and Savior (2 Pet. 1:11; 3:18). In Jesus, we are called not only to bring His gracious love, healing, and deliverance to all the nations as Savior, but also to bring His glory and government as Lord and King. Jesus has commissioned us to *"teach and make disciples"* of all the people of the earth (Matt. 28:19 NET/KJV). What are we called to teach? We are to *"teach these new disciples **to obey all the [love] commands**"* of Jesus (TLB). He is the King of kings and Lord of lords; no one is exempt from His lordship and love.

This book continues where the first book, *The War Songs of God*, leaves off. The first book on the War Songs lays the foundation, and this book on the Lock and Load Prophecies is the next step as the Spirit and power of God cause us to march on the heads of our enemies.

I highly encourage you, if you have not already, to read *The War Songs of God* first. It introduces and explains the concepts on how we gain the victory through singing the War Songs in the Word of God: songs specifically designed by God to tear down spiritual strongholds. The War Songs and other songs of victory are explained in *The Lock and Load Prophecies of God*.

The Fivefold Purpose of Prophecy

As we study the Lock and Load prophecies of God, we must first understand the purpose of prophecy. The final outcome of prophecy is to reveal Jesus and Him alone to us and to the world. When the Apostle John receives the revelation from an angel about the *marriage supper of the Lamb,* he falls at the angel's feet to worship him.

The angel rebukes John and tells him not to worship him, for he is a fellow servant along with John and all believers. The angel admonishes John, *"Do not do it! ... Worship God!* **For the purpose of all prophecy ... is to tell about Jesus"** (Rev. 19:10 NIV/TLB). The angel reveals to John the purpose of all prophecy is to tell us about Jesus.

Two other Bible translations read, *"For the testimony of Jesus is the spirit of prophecy"* (NASB) and ***"the essence of prophecy is to give a clear witness for Jesus"*** (NLT). The purpose and focus of all prophecy, in both the Old and the New Testaments, is to clearly reveal Jesus to us and the world.

The purpose of prophecy is to give us a clear picture of Jesus

There are five major purposes for prophecy in the Bible. They are:

- **Communicate** future events to warn and direct God's people: God warns Noah of the coming flood and instructs him to build an ark for his family and the animals (Gen. 6:11-22). Peter tells us that Noah was *"a preacher of righteousness, the sole voice of righteousness (who)* **warned the world** *of God's righteous judgment"* (2 Pet. 2:5 MSG/NLT/NLV). Noah was a prophetic preacher. His ark was a picture of Jesus, Who today is our Ark of mercy and protection in God's new age of grace.

- **Comfort and Courage** for Believers: Paul in his first letter to the Church at Corinth explains this purpose, *"**He who prophesies**, preaching the message of God, **is helping others grow in the Lord, encouraging and comforting them**"* (1 Cor. 14:3 RSV/TLB). Prophecy directs us to Jesus, Who always extends His grace to us, building us up with His courage and comfort.

- **Convict and Convert** Unbelievers: Paul reveals this goal of prophecy later in the same chapter, *"**If all of you are prophesying**, and unbelievers or people who don't understand these things come into your meeting, **they will be convicted of sin**, and **called into account by all**, the plain words will bring them up against the truth. As* *they listen, their secret thoughts will be laid bare, and **they will fall down with their face to the ground and worship God, declaring. 'God is really among you!'"*** (1 Cor. 14:24-25 NLT/NRSV/MSG/NET). Prophecy opens our eyes to a full revelation of Jesus and shows us not only His mercy and forgiveness but also His righteousness, holiness, and glory.

- **Confront and Correct rebellion and idolatry** first in God's people and then in the world: When the nation of Israel continued to harden her heart to the Lord and follow false gods, He sent Jeremiah to prophesy of Israel's 70 years of captivity, but after the 70 years were over the Lord would return them to their land (Jer. 25:4-13). As Daniel read this prophecy, he interceded for Israel and the angel Gabriel came and promised him the Lord would *"restore and rebuild Jerusalem"* (Dan. 9:25 KJV/NLT).

- **Condemn and Consume** demonic strongholds: An example would be the Lord's Lock and Load prophecies. God gives Ezekiel prophetic words against the city of Tyre in chapters 26 – 28. The prophecy was not just against *"the **prince** of Tyre"* (Ezek. 28:2 NKJV), but especially against *"the **king** of Tyre"* (Ezek. 28:12 NKJV). This king was *"the anointed angel ... who lived in the Garden of Eden"* (Ezek. 28:13-14 CW). He was the *"Evil One who works behind the scenes ... through men like the prince of Tyre"* (CW). The devil was the king, the true ruler, while the prince was just a man, a puppet in the enemy's hands. God's Lock and Load Prophesies address these spiritual principalities and powers ruling in high places to destroy them.

As our Commander and Chief, Jesus always leads us in triumph. It is vital for pastors, preachers, intercessors, and worship leaders to get this revelation of the power released in God's prophetic Word Weapons as we preach, pray, prophecy, and praise Him. We overcome all the power of the evil one as we sing God's songs of victory in our corporate praise and worship.

> *Jesus, as our Commander-in-Chief always leads us in His victory*

The five purposes of the spirit of prophecy testify of Jesus as the Prophet, Priest, and King of the world. The first purpose listed above testifies of Jesus as the Prophet communicating and guiding His people what to do especially during hard times. The second and third purposes testify of Jesus as our Great High Priest convicting, converting, and comforting His children as He brings them into His home. The fourth and fifth purposes of prophecy testify of Jesus as King, ruling over all the earth as He corrects their rebellion, but Jesus is also Lord over the principalities and powers in high places as He confronts and destroys their strongholds. Jesus is Lord over all! He has won the victory in every area of life, and the Spirit of prophecy reveals these wonderful truths.

The focus of this book is to fulfill the fourth and fifth purposes of prophecy. *The Lock and Load Prophecies of God* is the result of studying over a hundred such prophecies in the Bible (See Appendix A). As we proclaim these specific prophecies they bring forth the defeat, death, and destruction of the Lord's demonic adversaries. As we sing, shout, and stand on God's words of victory, we'll see every enemy put under the feet of King Jesus. This includes them being put under our feet as well, because the Church is the body of Christ (Eph. 1:20-23).

David prophesied, *"The LORD said unto my Lord, 'sit at My right hand **until** I make Your enemies a footstool for Your feet'"* (Psa. 110:1 NIV). Jesus will sit at the right hand of the Father God **until** the Father has placed every enemy under Jesus' feet. Because every believer is part of the body of Christ; that means that every enemy will also be placed under our feet.

The Apostle Paul encouraged the church at Rome with this truth, **"The God of peace will soon crush satan under your feet. He will swiftly pound satan to a pulp under your feet.** *And the wonderful favor of our Lord Jesus will surround you. Enjoy the best of Jesus!"* (Rom. 16:20 NKJV/MSG/tPt). What a glorious promise! There is no greater peace than having the enemy *under our feet* because of the grace and power we have in Jesus.

> There is no greater peace than when God crushes satan under our feet

ENDNOTE

1. The word *thriambeuo* at: http://www.blbclassic.org/lang/lexicon/lexicon.cfm?Strongs=G2358&t=KJV.

Why Read This Book?

Why should anyone read this book—especially one with a militaristic title about taking Old Testament prophecies to "lock and load" them like bullets into a gun? Well, this book is for anyone who desires to see God's kingdom of love, life, and peace overwhelm the evil one's kingdom of cruelty, death, and chaos.

In the Bible, God has given His people specific Words to use as weapons to demolish every onslaught of the devil. The Lord makes available to us His supernatural weapons so we, by the power of His Holy Spirit, can tear down these demonic strongholds. Here are a few of the strongholds of hate and chaos covered in this book God has called us to destroy:

- Groups like ISIS terrorizing the land with their cruel violence and death.

- The sex trade capturing young girls and boys, and selling as slaves for sexual pleasure.

- Racial tension in the USA and in many other countries ready to erupt in chaos.

- Continual conflict in the Middle East between Israel and the Arab nations.

- The spirit of poverty and failure overwhelming families in every area of the globe.

- Lives assaulted with shame: full of disappointment, frustration, and hopelessness.

- Sexual perversions and addictions that enslave and ruin hearts and homes.

- These are just a few examples of the works of darkness infecting our nation and every nation in the world.

This book covers Old Testament prophecies God declared against nations, many of which no longer exist, but these prophecies are very important for us to study and understand. These words are vital because even though those nations may no longer exist, the demonic forces which ruled over them in the past are still there and active today. These principalities and powers are found in other regions as well and still enslaving nations. It's time for them to fall.

What these spiritual weapons are and how we use them is what *The Lock and Load Prophecies of God* is all about. This book is written for everyone who wants to take up their weapon and bring the victory of Jesus to our world. To destroy strongholds so the love and life of God's glory cover the Earth as the waters cover the sea.

Jesus commands us, *"Now go **in My authority** and make disciples of all nations"* (Matt. 28:19 tPt). We must go in His authority to have the power to cast down the strongholds. Because we'll never disciple the nations until we first destroy the strongholds over them. This divine call is not a call to works; it's God's call for us to love the nations. The whole reason we fight is because we are compelled by the love of Jesus. God's army is full of His *love warriors*. This is why you should read this book.

IF YOU HAVE NO DESIRE TO FIGHT
AS GOD'S WARRIORS OF LOVE THEN
PUT THIS BOOK BACK ON THE SHELF
AND BUY SOMETHING ELSE

INTRODUCTION

MEANT FOR GOD'S WARRIORS OF LOVE

"Let the weak say, 'I am a strong warrior!'"

Joel 3:10 KJV/NRSV

IT'S TIME TO GO TO WAR!

A war is raging all around us. It is a war so encompassing, that it touches not only every person on earth but touches heaven itself (Rev. 12:7)[1]. If there is a conflict in the heavenlies, then know most assuredly that our world cannot go unscaled. We are also affected. It is time for the Body of Christ to ask God to train our hands for battle as He did David for warfare worship. David declares, *"**You've trained me with the weapons of warfare-worship**: Now I'll descend down into battle with power, to chase and conquer my foes"* (Psa. 18:34 tPt). Lord teach us how to overcome the dragon and his cohorts (Rev. 12:11). It is time for the children of God to enlist in His army, become His trained warriors of love and go to war.

There is an adversary, and many believers are trying to ignore him, hoping he will go away, but he will not go away. The evil one will gladly place his foot on our neck and walk all over our back as he oppresses us, our children, and our country. It's time to put a stop to his cruel dominion. It's time to place every demonic enemy under the feet of Jesus.

For Jesus has given us *"all authority and power to tread on serpents and scorpions.* **You will trample upon every demon before you and overcome every power satan possesses;** *and nothing shall by any means hurt you as you walk in this authority"* (Luke 10: 19 KJV/tPt). Whatever we, as the Church, have been doing for the last two hundred years is not working. It's time to seek God and find out how to do things His way.

> Whatever the church has been doing for the last 200 years is not working, it's time to seek God and do the things His way

God has an army, and He has enlisted us. Paul calls a fellow believer named Archippus, *"our **fellow soldier of the cross** [in the Christian warfare],* **our brother in God's army**, *who fights the same battle with [us]"* Phm 1:2 (NLT/Amp/BBE/Knox). All believers are like Archippus; whether we realize it or not, we're all soldiers in the Army of God. The Lord has an army because He has adversaries that oppose His will and rule.[2]

At the beginning of the book of Psalms we are warned about these adversaries of the Lord, *"What has provoked the nations to embrace anger and chaos? Leaders of nations stand united; rulers put their heads together,* **plotting against the Eternal One and His Anointed King, trying to figure out how they can throw off the gentle reign of God's love, step** *out from under the restrictions of His claims to advance their own schemes"* (Psa. 2:1-3 Voice). As a result of this resistance to the Lord, all believers have the honor of being enlisted in God's military service. What are we called to do in His army? We don't go into a physical battle like in the crusades. No! We go into a violent "holy war" in the Spirit against the forces of darkness.

One answer is in Psalm 149. There we are directed to sing a *"New Song"* (vs. 1) as we address the enemies of God. Know this promise of God; plant it deep within your soul, *"Let His faithful followers* **erupt in praise, singing triumphantly wherever they are***, even as they lie down for sleep in the evening. God's high and holy praises fill their mouths,* **for their shouted praises are their weapons of war!** *These warring weapons will bring vengeance on every opposing force and every resistant power who denies God.* **To bind their kings with chains,** *their nobles will be locked up with fetters of iron.* **This is the honor for all His godly lovers who serve Him"** (Psa. 149:5-9 RSV/Voice/tPt/NAB). It is not physical kings and rulers that we are bind by the power of God. It is the spiritual forces in high places working behind those rulers. It is our honor, as we worship Jesus, that the evil ones are bound in chains.

The whole book of Psalms is mainly one big collection of victory songs we're called to sing as we triumph in Christ, our Messiah. Jesus said *"**This is war, and there is no neutral ground.** If you're not on My side, you're the enemy; if you are not helping, you're making things worse"* (Luke 11:23 MSG). Jesus echoes the words of Job who said, *"**Human life on earth is like serving in the army,***

> As we worship the Lord Jesus, it is our honor that the powers in high places are bound with God's chains

the life of man is a battle, warfare." (Job 7:1a CJB/DRB). It's time for us to get on the Lord's side and go into battle.

The Marine Corps Never Taught Us Fear

In all of our training, not once did the Marine Corps teach us to be afraid. They taught us to be confident and courageous as we faced our fears. How we need this truth in the Body of Christ!

Hear Paul's exhortation, **"Be brave when you face your enemies**, *in nothing terrified by your adversaries.* **Your courage** *will show them that they are going to be destroyed, and it will show you that you will be saved. God will make all of this happen"* (Phil. 1:28 CEV/CEB). We go to war in faith, not fear. We fear no consequences. Our courage is a *clear sign* to the enemy of their coning destruction. We fight with courage because we have confidence in the power of our God through the finished work of Jesus on the Cross.

Paul concludes, *"It is now your turn to take part in this battle you once saw me engaged in, and which, in point of fact I am still fighting"* (Phil. 1:30 Phil). As we go into this battle we are not *"paralyzed in any way by what your opponents are doing"* (Phil. 1:28 Voice). It's time to take part in the battle.

Remember, I am coming from the perspective of a military service member. When I mention fighting demons in spiritual warfare, many believers hold back. They warn me saying, "Hold on brother that's dangerous." My response, "If the Marines never trained me to be afraid, how much more courageous should the army of God be." We attack with confidence in Jesus, in the weapons He provides us, and in His strategies of war.

FOUR BASIC INSTRUCTIONS FROM BOOT CAMP

Before we go further we must understand a few things about spiritual warfare. What applies to combat for a physical army directly applies to God's spiritual army. We can look at how the military trains its soldiers for our guidance. Here are the vital, main points:

1. **Know your weapon:**

   Everyone who has enlisted in the military knows this first rule by heart. As warriors in the Army of God, we must know that the first and foremost weapon in our arsenal to use against demonic principalities and powers is the Word of God. John the Beloved tells us that *"they overcame him [the devil] by the Blood of the Lamb, and by **the word** of their testimony; and they loved not their lives even in the face of death"* (Rev. 12:11 KJV/MLB). This is a very important key to victory.

   A more accurate translation would be "by the Word **in** their testimony." It is not just any words we speak. It's the Word of God in our testimony that gives us the victory. Two versions translate this idea clearly: *"they overcame him by **the preaching** of the Word"* (Noli) and by *"**the Message** to which they bore testimony"* (TCNT). It is the Word of God which we confess overcomes the evil one. It is not our words that give us the victory; it is God's Word.

Jesus gives us this example when He faced satan's temptations in the wilderness. Each time Jesus repels the devil's attack, He does so by responding with the Word of God. Each time Jesus responds with, *"It is written;" "It is written;" "It is written."* (Matt. 4:1-11 & Luke 4:1-14). He corrects accusation with revelation. We'd do well to follow Jesus' example.

When our adversary comes against us the first thing he wants to find out how much of the Word of God do we really know. When he tempted Eve in the garden he asks her *"Has God said?"* (Gen. 3:1). In other words, satan was basically asking Eve, "Do you know the Word of God?" And not only do you know His Word, do you understand His Word? Remember Jesus' parable of the Sower. The seed of the Word of God must not only be planted deep within our hearts; it must also be *understood* so that it can't be stolen by the wicked one (Matt. 13:18-19). We only own what we understand, and that revelation can never be taken away from us.

Jesus explains the seeds, the Word of God, that falls on the wayside, *"When anyone hears the word about the kingdom and **does not understand it**, the evil one comes and **snatches what was sown in his heart**; this is the seed sown by the wayside"* (Matt. 13:19 NET/KJV). The Word had been planted in their heart and yet the enemy could steal it because they did not understand it. The Pharisees knew the Word of God in their mind, but they definitely did not know and understand the God of the Word in their heart. We must have both the Word and the revelation to overcome.

2. **Match your weapon to your warfare:**

   To address this second point we need to take a little Bible quiz. When Jesus was tested in the wilderness by satan, He responds with specific words to defeat each of the devil's temptations. We resist the enemy with the Word of God, but that Word must address and nullify that specific attack.

   ## Match Jesus' acclamations against the devil's accusations:

___ *turn these stones into bread*	a. *do not tempt the Lord your God*
___ *cast Yourself; the angels will protect you*	b. *worship the Lord only*
___ *bow down and worship me (i.e. satan)*	c. *man shall live by the Word of God*

   The answers are c, a, and b. Notice there is a Divine Acclamation for every Demonic Accusation that comes against us. As we match God's Word answers to their correct counterpart, we see that Jesus matched His word weapon to the specific warfare He faced. We will never conquer unless we follow Jesus' example!

   So when we are in a spiritual battle we need to know all the weapons the Lord has provided for us and how to use them. In the natural realm, if two armies are in a firefight where each side only has rifles, the battle will

   There is a Divine acclamation against every demonic accusation

be won by those who are the best warriors and leaders. But if one army shows up with a tank, the soldiers on the other side must quickly change their tactics and weapons! They grab the soldier with the RPG (rocket propelled grenade) launcher, the weapon specifically designed for tanks, and take that tank out of commission. This is the same tactic we need to use in our spiritual battles.

3. **Stay within your sphere of authority:**

   In the natural realm a four-member rifle team does not attack a whole Company or a Division composed of hundreds or thousands of troops. Yes, there are exceptions in the Bible where a small group would take on a much larger opponent and win, such as Gideon's army of 300 defeating the thousands of the host of Midian (Judges 7:6-25) but wisdom in spiritual warfare would have us remain within the area of our responsibility. Don't bite off more than we can chew. The larger the stronghold we're coming against; the larger our army needs to be.

   Here are some examples to explain what I mean. Parents are responsible for their children and therefore have the authority to cover them in prayer. A Church has responsibility to not just cover their members in prayer, but to pray for their city. God's wisdom would have them to join with other churches in their town to pray for their town. It grows from there; the bigger the area to pray for, the larger the spiritual army that's required.

   Churches from many cities would join together to pray for their state, and Churches from many states would join together to pray for their nation and the nations of the world. Bottom line: if you are a member of a small prayer group say of 10-15 people, wisdom would not lead you take on the stronghold over a whole nation. It would be smart to join with others to take on that large of an opponent.

4. **Know your adversaries:**

    Paul instructs us to not be *"ignorant of the schemes of the evil one"* so the devil cannot *"outwit and take advantage of us"* (2 Cor. 2:11 KJV/GW). The Message Bible tells us that we must know the enemies' tactics, so we don't *"unwittingly give satan an opening for yet more mischief — [because] we're not oblivious to his sly ways."* Here is a very important word of wisdom. We are not into demonology, the study of demons. We do not focus on the works of the devil. No. Our focus and concentration is on Jesus and His work.

    Paul again warns us *"Learn how to please the Lord. Have nothing to do with the bad things done in darkness. Instead, show that these things are wrong.* **It is shameful and disgraceful to even mention and talk about these things done in secret"** (Eph. 5:10-12 NLV/NASB/NLT). I desire to follow his advice in this book.

    I'll say just enough about our adversaries to expose their deceptions and lies but won't focus on, or go into detail on, what they are doing. It is *shameful and disgraceful to talk about* what the devil is doing. Instead, we'll talk about the love of our God and glorify what Jesus is doing! All we need is God's discernment that something is a work of the evil one; we don't need to study it in detail. Once we're warned; we call upon Jesus for His wisdom on how to destroy it.

    Jesus has commissioned us to *"go and make disciples of all nations"* (Matt. 28:19 NIrV). This command to disciple the nations, is a call to go into spiritual battle to win the hearts and minds of the world. We will never disciple the nations, until we first destroy the strongholds holding them captive.

A SPIRITUAL BATTLE

Because we are spiritual warriors, in a spiritual battle, we must use spiritual weapons. The Lock and Load prophecies of God are some of His most powerful weapons in the Spirit. They are the powerful, divine Words that we proclaim in our testimony that overcome the devil (Rev. 12:11).

> *Because we are spiritual warriors in a spiritual battle, we must use spiritual weapons*

The Apostle John tells us that even young people have defeated the devil because the Word of God is in their hearts, *"Young people, I am writing to you, because* ***you are strong. God's message is firm in your hearts*** *and you have defeated the evil one"* (1 John 2:14b CEV).

We are strong, Army of God Strong. When the Word of God is firm in our hearts, then we can defeat the evil one. Put the Word of God's Lock and Load Prophecies firmly in our heart and with faith release God's power as they come out of our mouth!

John goes on and tells us *"Little children, you are from God,* ***and have conquered them;*** *because He, the Holy Spirit, Who is in you, is greater than the spirit who is in the world"* (1 John 4:4 NKJV/NLT/NRSV). Who is this spirit living in the world that we have conquered? Just read the verse right before this to find out, ***"And this is the spirit of the antichrist,*** *which you have heard was coming, and **is now already in the world*** (1 John 4:3 NKJV). The Holy Spirit in us is greater than the spirit of the antichrist that is in the world.

Don't tell me that in the last days the antichrist will rise up and take over the world. The Word of God tells me that the Holy Spirit in one of God's *little children* is greater than and will conquer anyone moving by the spirit of the antichrist in the world.

IT'S TIME TO GO TO WAR!

ENDNOTES

1. This is not the third heaven that Paul talked about, where the throne of the Lord is located (2 Cor. 12:2), for satan was cast out of that realm long ago when he rebelled against the Lord (Isa. 14:12). There are three levels of heaven: a. the first level includes the physical sky with the clouds and wind, b. the second level includes the universe of the sun, moon and stars, and c. the third level includes the place where the throne of God and His angels are located. This term refers to the first level of heaven, where the enemy roams as the prince and power of *the air* (Eph. 2:2 KJV). Jesus gives us a glorious revelation when He tells His disciples that wherever the Gospel of the Kingdom is preached with power that the devil is cast down from his place of authority in that region, *"And He said unto them, 'I watched how satan fell, like lightning **from the sky'"*** (Luke 10:18 NEB/Rieu).

2. John tells us in the book of Revelation that there are three demonic leaders leading the spiritual assault against God's people. **Leviathan** is *"the monster or the beast from **the sea**"* (Rev. 13:1-10 with Isa. 27:1 NIV), **Behemoth** is the *"beast coming out of **the earth**"* (Rev. 13:11-18 with Job 40:15-24), and the *"**great red Dragon**"* who *"appeared… **in heaven**"* (Rev. 12:3). It is interesting that there are three beasts who lead this spiritual attack: Behemoth from the land, Leviathan from the sea and the Dragon from the air. It just so happens that there are three main branches of military in the

United States: the Army, the Navy and the Air Force. The Marines are a special department of the Navy, who attack from the land, sea, and air.

We are all enlisted as warriors in one of God's spiritual, Special Forces. God's Army comprises His ground forces of Evangelists, Pastors and Teachers against Behemoth. They plant the seeds of the words of salvation into the soil, the hearts of the people. God's Navy patrols the seas. The Hebrew word for sea is *yam* and many times represents chaos (Retrieved at: http://www.newworldencyclopedia.org/entry/Yam_%28god%29). So God's Navy is composed of His Prophets, those called to control the chaos of Leviathan. They do so with God's waters of baptism and the baptism in the Holy Ghost. Demonic attacks by the Dragon from the heavens are repulsed by God's Divine Air Force consisting of His Apostles, Intercessory Prayer Warriors and our praise and worship. We are in one of these groups. Let's find our place and stand against the works of the evil one.

And then some of you are Marines. You can go anywhere, guarding the land, the sea and the air. You're trained and equipped, ready to go fight wherever God needs you!

VOLUME ONE

The Lock and Load Prophecies of God

*"But praise be to God,
Who always causes us to triumph in Christ;
Who makes us strong to overcome;
Who grants us complete success as we sing songs of victory."*

2 Cor. 2:14 CTB/BBE

CHAPTER ONE

RELEASING THE ROAR AND PEACE OF GOD

*"The Lord roars from Zion, **'Lock and Load!'**"*

Amos 1:2 CTB

GET READY TO FIGHT AS WE SING AND DANCE UNTO THE LORD!

We must discern the invisible battle raging around us. Many believers are in the center of the hurricane swirling around them, totally unaware of this spiritual storm. The war may be invisible, but its devastating effects are clearly evident! We see its destructive force everywhere: personally in our lives and homes, locally, nationally, and even internationally.

God calls us to war against these spiritual attacks in our warfare worship. Judah and King Jehoshaphat taught us the power of praise, for *"as soon as they began to sing their joy and their loud shouts of praise were heard, the Lord laid an ambush ... and [Judah's enemies] began to destroy each other"*

(2 Chron. 20:22-23 KJV/JB/NEB/NAB). The psalmist Asaph cries out, *"Lord, just singing about You makes me strong! So I'll keep shouting for joy to Jacob's God, My Champion!"* (Psa. 81:1 tPt). And David declares, *"You've trained me with the weapons of warfare-worship; now I'll descend down into battle with power to chase and conquer my foes. You empower me for victory with Your wrap-around presence"* (Psa. 18:34-35a tPt). What beautiful reasons why we never let anything stop our praise and warfare worship!

Going back to Psalm 81 God responds to David, *"You called out to Me in your time of trouble and I rescued you ... **I came down to save you** ... I am your only God, the Living God! **Wasn't I the One who broke the strongholds over you and raised you out of bondage?** Open your mouth with a mighty decree, I will fulfill it now, you'll see! The words that you speak, so shall it be!"* (Psa. 81:7a & 10 tPt). Once the Lord has destroyed the strongholds over us, He can now work through us to break the strongholds over others. Let this mighty cycle of victory begin!

> We should hear about what Jesus is doing on the world news and local news every night

Whatever the Church has been doing for the last two hundred years is not working. When Jesus comes to a town, *"the whole world runs after Him"* (John 12:19 NIV/NET). And as Jesus' followers obey Him, they turn *"the world upside down"* (Acts 17:6 NKJV). If we were doing this, we'd hear about Jesus and the acts of His Spirit on the world and local news every night.

Never forget the kind of spiritual warfare the Lord is calling us into. It is not so much the screaming and shouting "rock 'em, sock 'em" combat that many of us have experienced, but rather it's the *pleasantness of worship* that He's calling us to participate in. So many times it's the gentlest worship that is the most deadly to our demonic adversaries.

Listen to David as he rejoices before the Lord, *"You have built a stronghold **by the songs of babies. Strength rises up with the chorus of singing children.** This kind of praise has the power to shut satan's mouth. **Childlike worship will silence the madness** of those who oppose You."* (Psa. 8:2 tPt). It is when we and our children with us sing and dance to such songs as, *"Dance with Me Oh Lover of My Soul"* by Jesus Culture that every enemy is crushed under our feet. They are beaten as we worship at the footstool, the Mercy-seat of our God. Please keep this vital aspect of praise, worship, and dance in mind as we study the Lock and Load Prophecies of God.

> The songs of babies shut satan's mouth, childlike worship silences madness

WHAT THE TERM LOCK AND LOAD MEANS

Before we begin, we need to know what the phrase Lock and Load means. It's a military command used in combat. It refers to making your weapon battle ready. It's when a military leader commands us to *lock* a magazine (a clip of ammunition) into our weapon and *load* a round or a bullet into the chamber. Now, we and our weapon are ready to attack. All we have to do is aim, pull the trigger, and fire. In spiritual warfare, our ammunition is the *spoken* Word of God.

The Word of God is a sword. It is *"the mighty razor-sharp **Spirit-sword of the spoken Word of God**"* (Eph. 6:17 tPt). But it never becomes a sword until we confess it out of our mouths. Jesus says, *"I will fight against them with **the sword of My mouth**"* (Rev. 2:16 KJV). One version reads. *"I will contend with such men with **words that will cut like a sword**"* (TCNT). We fire away whenever we speak, shout, and sing God's Word. It cuts down the enemy like a sword. The Word of God becomes a sword, not when we just read it or think it, but when we confess it. When the Word of God comes out of your mouth, it changes into the sword of God.

Lock and Load Prophecies Release the Roar of God

There are whole sections in the Bible where the Spirit of prophecy falls on God's prophet, and they begin to proclaim the Word of the Lord upon the nations. An excellent example is Amos (an Old Testament prophet) when he cries out, *"The Lord **roars** from Zion, His voice **thunders** from Jerusalem."* (Amos 1:2 GW). God is preparing Amos to give His prophetic Word against the nations around Israel as well as against Israel and Judah. The Divine Warrior roars His command to Amos, *"**Lock and Load!** Prepare to fire away with My Word."* The Lock and Load Prophecies are specific words of prophesy that release the roar of the Lord in the Spirit against His enemies. If we use anything else, we'll be slaughtered.

> *In spiritual warfare our ammunition is the word of God*

The purpose of God's roar is to set His people free. The prophet Hosea reveals the heart of God as

He comes to release His children from their captivity. See what happens when God roars! During Hosea's day the people of Israel were slaves to the spirits of sorcery and seduction of Assyria. They were in such bondage by their sins that they were unable to return to the Lord. Hosea proclaims God's message, **"Their deeds will not permit them to return to their God. They couldn't turn to God if they wanted to because a spirit of adultery controls their heart. They wouldn't recognize God if they saw Me"** (Hosea 5:4 AAT/WYC/NET/MSG). The only way they can be released from this spiritual entrapment is by the roar of the Lord, and He's coming to deliver them!

The Lord cries out: *"I won't punish you in My anger, and I won't destroy Israel again. I am God and not a human; I am the Holy One, and I am among you. I will not come against you in anger. They (i.e. Israel) will go after [follow] the Lord and* **He will roar like a lion at their enemies. When He roars, His children will hurry to Him** *from the west. They will come swiftly like birds from Egypt and like doves from Assyria.* **'I will settle them again in their homes,'** **says the Lord;** *this is a promise, the very word from the Lord"* (Hosea 11:9-11 EXB/TLB/NEB). When the Lord roars against our enemies, their chains over us are broken, and we are free.

God's roar is like a singer who hits a certain note, usually a high C, and shatters a glass. The frequency of that specific note can shatter a crystal glass.[1] The roar of God is released in His Word, and the specific prophecy against that specific stronghold is set at just the exact frequency in the Spirit required to

> *The prophecies of God are set at the exact frequency in the Spirit required to shatter spiritual strongholds*

shatter those demonic chains! No chain of the evil one can withstand the power of God's roar. Once we are free, like birds out of the snare we fly back to Him. He resettles us in our homes. This is a sure promise to us from the Lord.

GOD'S PROPHECY RELEASES GOD'S ROAR

There is a direct connection between prophecy and the roar of God. Amos says, *"The Lion has **roared**—who will not fear? The Lord God has spoken, who can but **prophecy**?"* (Amos 3:8 KJV/TLB). When God directs us to tear down the walls of a demonic stronghold, like the War Cry shouted at the battle of Jericho (Josh. 6:20), we prophecy and release His roar!

This book is a Bible study of over 100 prophecies in the Old and New Testaments (See Appendix A for a complete list). They are the Word Weapons the Lord has given to us to destroy the work of the devil and all his demonic strongholds. In this book we'll study the *"It is written"* found in God's Word to proclaim against these spiritual forces and overcome them. As the Lord's warriors, He has called us to attack, kill, and bury our demonic adversaries.

God's Lock and Load prophecies are His battle-ready Word ammunition to fire into the camp of the evil one. As we speak (evangelism), shoot (intercessory prayer), shout (preaching and prophesying), and sing (praise and worship) these prophetic words, we send forth His Words like arrows of flaming glory that explode in the camps of the enemy throughout the world. The power of God is released as we praise, preach, pray, and prophecy His Word.

When God says it's time to attack, to Lock and Load, all we do is aim, pull the trigger and fire, and the power of God strikes that specific demonic stronghold He's ordering us to tear down. Jesus is calling us to do His work. As we work with Him we *"destroy, loosen, and dissolve the works of the devil"* (1 John 3:8 AMP). One of the most powerful ways to do this is through the Word of God in His Lock and Load prophesies.

Examples of Lock and Load Prophecies

All four Major Prophets of the Old Testament—Isaiah, Jeremiah, Ezekiel, and Daniel—have entire sections where the prophet releases God's Word against the nations that opposed Israel. In Volume One we'll explain in detail what Lock and Load Prophecies are. In Volume Two, we'll study many of these prophecies the Old Testament prophets proclaimed against their demonic oppressors, and how they apply to us. These spiritual strongholds still exist today and must be torn down.

The sections where the four Major Prophets addressed these strongholds are:

1. Isaiah—Chapters 13-25, 30, 34, 46
2. Jeremiah—Chapters 46-51
3. Ezekiel—Chapters 25-35
4. Daniel—Chapters 2-7, 11
    (See Appendix A for a detailed list.)

There are whole sections in their writings where the Spirit of God falls upon the prophet and they fire away at the forces of wickedness in high places who are controlling those nations.

Then there are the twelve Minor Prophets. They are called minor only because they are shorter in length than the four Major Prophets. Eight of the twelve Minor Prophets also have whole sections where God roars and addresses Israel's adversaries. We will also cover in Volume Two some of these Lock and Load prophecies of the Minor Prophets which are listed below:

1. Amos—Chapters 1-2
2. Obadiah—Chapter 1
3. Jonah—Chapter 3
4. Nahum—Chapters 1-3
5. Habakkuk—Chapters 1-3
6. Zephaniah—Chapters 1-3
7. Zechariah—Chapters 9-14
8. Malachi—Chapters 1-4 *(See Appendix A.)*

Some of the strongholds the Lord roars against are over the nations of Babylon, Assyria, Egypt, Philistia, Moab, Ammon, Syria, Cush, Edom, Arabia, and Tyre, as well as Israel and Judah. God has not called us to sit around passively and watch the world go to hell in a hand basket. No! He commands us to go on the offensive and attack our adversary. We are called to join with Jesus and destroy the works of the devil, to *do even greater works"* (John 14:12 KJV/Phillips). One of the greater works is that we don't just attack the enemy, but we'll also discover that God commands us to kill and bury those demons as well!

> *God has not called us to passively watch as the world goes to hell in a hand basket. No, He commands us to attack, kill, and bury our demonic adversaries.*

A good example of battle ready, Lock and Load prophecies are given by Amos. He fires off a series of prophetic words against the nations around Israel and even against the strongholds holding Judah and Israel in bondage. Be patient and you will see how these ancient words from the past are just as vital and relevant for us to know and use today. Why? Because the same demonic spirits that operated during the days of Amos and all the other Old Testament prophets are alive and active today. It's past the time for them to be cast down and fall to the ground.

Amos declares, **"The Lord like a ferocious lion roars from Zion *and thunders from His Temple in Jerusalem"* (Amos 1:2 NEB/TLB). God cries out to Amos, "Lock and Load!" and Amos fires away:

> "Thus says the LORD, 'For three transgressions of **Tyre**, *even for four, I will not turn back My wrath …* **Therefore I will send fire upon the walls of Tyre and consume all her fortresses'"** (1:9 - 10 NIV/NASB/HCSB).

> "Thus says the LORD, 'For three transgressions of **Edom**, *even for four, I will not turn back My wrath …* **Therefore I will send fire … that will consume the fortresses of Bozrah'"** (1:11-12 NIV/NASB/HCSB).

> "Thus says the LORD, for three transgressions of **Ammon**, *even for four, I will not turn back My wrath …* **Therefore**

> ***I will send fire on the walls of Rabbah that will consume her fortresses'"*** (1:13-14 NIV/NASB/HCSB).

> *"Thus says the LORD, for three transgressions of **Moab**, even for four, I will not turn back My wrath ... **Therefore I will send fire upon Moab that will consume the fortresses of Kerioth'"*** (2:1-2 NIV/NASB/HCSB).

With these spiritual Word weapons, Amos fires away like a spiritual big game hunter, "Bam! Woe to you Tyre, Bam! Woe to you Edom, Bam! Woe to you Ammon, Bam! Woe to you Moab" BAM! BAM! BAM! The Holy Spirit roars through Amos as he prophesies the Word of the Lord at these cities and countries.

Never forget, the Word of God is not against the *people. It* is against the spiritual powers and principalities in high places controlling the people, the leaders of that nation. In Chapter Four on Jeremiah's prophesies, I'll explain in detail the powerful revelation in these Old Testament prophecies God has for us today.

GOD HAS NOT CALLED US TO BE "SONS OF THUNDER!"

Two of Jesus' disciples, were the brothers, James and John. Jesus called them the *"Sons of Thunder"* (Mark 3:17 KJV). This title can also be translated "sons of loud shouts (passionate)" or "sons of commotion (easily angered)" (tPt footnote). They were called this due to their intensity and zeal for the Lord.

But one time they got carried away as they reacted to a Samaritan village who refused to receive Jesus. In anger they asked Jesus, *"Lord, do You want us **to call down fire from heaven to burn them up**, like Elijah did?"* (Luke 9:54

NLT/MSG/NKJV). They thought this was a great idea, but what did Jesus say? *"But He turned and rebuked them, and said,* **'You do not understand what spirit it is you share. Don't you realize what comes from your hearts when you say that?** *For the Son of Man did not come to destroy men's lives, but to save them'"* (Luke 9:55-56 KJV/Knox/tPt/NASB). The spiritual, Holy Ghost fire that the Lord wants Amos to call down, is not literal fire.

The fire of God is a holy thing. The Lord commands us to love our enemies by pouring out the fire of God's love upon their heads. Paul said, *"Never pay back evil with evil ... if your enemy is hungry, feed him; if he is thirsty, give him something to drink, for in doing so you shall heap coals of fire upon his head"* (Rom. 12:17 & 20 NEB/KJV/TLB). Pouring coals of fire upon someone's head was an act of kindness. If someone's fire went out, they'd go around with a pan on their head asking their neighbors to share some live coals from their fire. By heaping coals of fire on their head you are helping them restart their fire so they could cook their supper.² As Daniel's three friends found out in the fiery furnace (Dan. 3:9-30), God's fire does not kill us: it heals us. The fire of God purifies us, promotes us, and sets us free.

> God's fire does not kill us; it heals us and sets us free

God is roaring not against the people, but against the principalities and powers in high places holding them captive. Look closer, and we see that the fire of God is coming, not upon the people but against the strongholds: the **walls**, the **gates**, the **fortresses** (See Amos 1:4, 10, 12, 14; 2:2). In other Bible versions these strongholds are called *"strong towers"* (EXB), *"forts"* (TLB), *"fortresses"* (GNT), *"citadels"* (HCSB), and *"strong-places"* (NLV). Can we see that God is saying these strongholds must come down?

The Hebrew word used here for forts, strong towers, etc. is *armown* and specifically refers to "the citadel of the palace, the highest, strongest part."³ God is coming against the citadel of that nation. What is a citadel? It is a fortress for the defense of a city. It is a "place of arms," where all the weapons are stored.⁴ It is the stronghold, the high place for that country, and God is all about destroying high places, the spiritual forts. He comes to shatter the unclean spirit that has a stranglehold over the leaders and people of every nation.

> God's lock and load prophecies are not against people; they are against principalities and powers in high places

Jesus is our example in destroying the works of the evil one. Jesus leads the way for He has *"disarmed the evil rulers and authorities. He shamed them publicly by His victory over them by the cross,"* and as a result we *"have died with Christ, and **He has set us free from the evil spirits of this world"*** (Col. 2:15 & 20 NLT/NET). These words reflect God's *Heart of War,* His warrior heart to set people free so they can come home to their Father.

Now, some would say, "Whoa brother, these are Old Testament prophecies. That's Old Covenant stuff. They are interesting as historical stories, but they do not apply to us today. We are now under the grace of God's New Covenant." If that's the case, then what do we do with the Lock and Load prophecies that Jesus declares as recorded in the Gospels of Matthew and Luke?

"Then Jesus began to rebuke the cities, He let fly on the cities where most of His miracles had been performed, because they did not repent from their sins and shrugging their shoulders went their own way. 'Woe to you Chorazin! Doom to you, Chorazin, what horrors await you! Woe to you Bethsaida, Doom Bethsaida, how terrible for you!

For if the miracles I did in you had been done in wicked Tyre and Sidon, their people would have repented of their sins and sat in deep repentance long ago, clothed in sackcloth and ashes. If they had seen half of the powerful miracles you have seen, they would have been on their knees in a minute. **I assure you, Tyre and Sidon will be better off on the Judgment Day than you. And you Capernaum, will you be lifted up to heaven? No, you will be brought down into hell,** *for if the works of power which were done in you had been done in Sodom, it would have remained until this day. I assure you, on the Judgment Day,* **Sodom will get off easy compared to you!"** (Matt. 11:20-24 and Luke 10:8-16 NLT/NIV/NKJV/NET/NASB/BBE/NRSV/MSG).

These words of warning and judgment given by Jesus sound just like the Lock and Load prophecies in the Old Covenant. Jesus declares that the three cities of Chorazin, Bethsaida, and Capernaum will have it worse than the three Old Testament cities of Sodom, Tyre, and Sidon because they have rejected the Son of God!

According to Jesus, Lock and Load prophecies are alive and well today in God's New Covenant of grace. We need them today! Now is the time to destroy the high places in the spirit that come against the Truth and revelation of Jesus. Remember what Paul said to the Church in Corinth: *"It is true that I am an ordinary, weak human being, but I don't use human plans and methods to win my battles.* **I use God's**

mighty weapons, *for these weapons are not worldly* **but have divine power to destroy the devil's strongholds.** *These weapons can break down every proud argument against God* **and every high wall** *that can be built to keep men from finding Him.* **With these weapons I can capture rebels and bring them back to God,** *and change them into men whose heart's desire is obedience to Christ"* (2 Cor. 10:3-5 TLB/KJV). This is our call *to destroy every stronghold and high wall* that has been set up to keep people from finding God. Notice that stronghold and wall are the same words used in Amos. Our mission is to destroy walls and strongholds, rescue rebels, bring them back to God, and change their heart's desire to obey Jesus.

> *God's mighty weapons have power to destroy every demonic stronghold*

Praise to God that includes these prophetic words along with our warfare worship and dance break down the strongholds of evil. Just as David danced before the Lord as he brought the Ark of the Covenant back into Jerusalem (1 Chron. 15), today in our worship and dance we usher in the presence of Jesus into a city, for the *"Desire of all nations"* has come (Hag. 2:7).

ENDNOTES

1. High C shatters glass at: http://www.scientificamerican.com/article/fact-or-fiction-opera-singer-can-shatter-glass/.
2. Heaping coals of fire on the head is an act of kindness at: https://dailygoodies.wordpress.com/2010/01/04/heaping-coals-of-fire-a-figure-of-speech/.
3. The word *armown* at: http://www.blbclassic.org/lang/lexicon/lexicon.cfm?Strongs=H759&t=KJV.
4. Noah Webster's 1828 Dictionary (Hardback Edition).

CHAPTER TWO

GOD'S PROGRESSION OF VICTORY

IN THE FOUR MAJOR PROPHETS

God has given this command concerning the evil one:
"I am digging your grave, and I will bury you,
for you are vile."
Nahum 1:14 CTB

LOCK AND LOAD PROPHECIES ARE AGAINST SPIRITUAL POWERS NOT PEOPLE

Ask the Lord to give you His Spirit of wisdom and revelation as you study His Truth. Make this your prayer: "Lord may *'the eyes of [my] heart be flooded with light, that [I] may know what is the hope of [Your] calling, and the richness of [Your] inheritance promised to [Your] people, and what is the **exceeding greatness of** [Your] **power in** [me as a]*

believers' (Eph. 1:18 KJV/Mont/Wey, brackets added). I ask for Your Spirit to give me the understanding of Your calling and the hope You have set before me. All of this is possible only by the exceeding greatness of Your power. It's never done by my power."

With this prayer in your heart, let us now begin our study. To prevent us from engaging in religious witchcraft, it is vital to understand this next principle. Yes, the Lock and Load prophecies in the Old Covenant were God's Word against the people and nations of that time. But these words have more meaning than that. God's purpose is to destroy the strongholds so He can set the people who are held captive to those spiritual forces free.

The Lock and Load Prophecies are Like Hell

The Lock and Load prophecies are like hell. God made hell, or *"the lake of fire"* for the devil and his demons (Rev. 20:11-15). God did not make the lake of fire for mankind. But if any one does not receive Jesus as Lord and have their name written in the Book of Life, the lake of fire will be their destiny along with the devil and the unclean spirits. So how are these prophecies like hell?

These prophecies are against the wicked forces in high places, the spirits controlling the leaders of those nations. The focus of God's Word is on that demon. If a leader repents and rejects the work of that demonic spirit, they'll be saved. But if that leader does not repent and return to the Lord, they will have to face the consequences of God along with that demon.

God does not desire humanity to suffer with the devil and unclean spirits. The Lord declares to the wicked men of Israel through the prophet Ezekiel, *"Say unto them, 'As surely as I live' declares the Sovereign Lord, **'I take no pleasure in the death of the wicked,** but rather that they turn from their wicked ways and live. **I take pleasure … in the wicked man's conversion that he may live.** Turn! Turn from your evil ways! O house of Israel, why should you die?'"* (Ezek. 33:11 NET/NAB/NEB). This is the heart of God.

> God takes pleasure in the conversion of wicked people-that they may live!

The Lord takes pleasure, not in the death and judgment of the wicked, but in their conversion. His desire is that they may live! Jesus says, *"Understand that it is never the desire or will of Your Father in Heaven, that one of these little ones should perish and be lost"* (Matt. 18:14 Rhm/Phillips). God's desire for the salvation of every man, woman, and child is the reason for His prophecies.

ALL FALSE GODS ARE DEMONS

The Lock and Load prophecies of God address the false gods, the demons, who are lording over and oppressing the nations. In the Psalms, David tells us that all the false gods of the nations are demons.[1] He proclaims, *"Great is the Lord and greatly to be praised, He is terrible to all the gods, **because all the gods of the nations are merely worthless demons. For all the gods of the heathen are devils,** but the Lord made the heavens"* (Psa. 96:4-5 NKJV/TLB/ISV/HCSB. Note: in NETS it is Psa. 95:5). We don't fight *against* people; we fight *for* the people, as we battle the false gods, the demonic strongholds over them. Our fight is not against flesh and blood; we don't fight people. Instead, we are commissioned to destroy demonic strongholds so people enslaved by them are delivered.

FALSE GODS OF EVERY NATION ARE WORTHLESS DEMONS

Paul tells us our battle is not against people but against principalities and powers in high places. He says, *"For we are not fighting against people made of flesh and blood,* **but against principalities, against powers, against the rulers of the darkness of who are now using their authority to try to rule this world. For they are a powerful class of demon-gods and evil spirits that hold this dark world in bondage.** *This is a life-or-death fight to the finish against the devil and all his angels"* (Eph. 6:12 TLB/NKJV/RRSV/CW/tPt/MSG). We're commissioned by God to engage in this life-or-death fight to the finish against the devil and all his angels.

This is why Paul goes on to exhort us that, *"You must put on the whole armor of God, in order* **that you may receive power to stand when evil attacks you, for you are destined for all things and will rise victorious"** (Eph. 6:13 CW/Rhm/tPt). We can only stand when we have put on the armor of God. Fighting evil forces with the arm of the flesh is spiritual suicide. Put on your armor! You're destined to rise victorious!

> To fight with the arm of flesh against the forces of evil is spiritual suicide

Paul reminds us, *"Indeed, we live as human beings and walk in the world; but we do not fight according to this world's rules of war.* **The weapons we fight with are not the weapons of this world.** *On the contrary,* **our weapons come from God; they are powered by God and effective at tearing down the** *devil's strongholds, for the destruction of **high places**, to demolish **fortresses** erected against His truth. With these weapons we tear down arguments. We use our powerful God-tools for smashing ideas, every proud, high-and-mighty philosophy that pits itself against the knowledge of the one true God; that keeps people from knowing God. **With these spiritual weapons energized with divine power we conquer their rebellious ideas, and we teach them to obey Christ**"* (2 Cor. 10:3-5 NRSV/VOICE/NLT/BBE/NIV/CW/NASB/tPt). Notice the word Paul uses is translated in different versions as: *strongholds, fortresses* and *high places.* Do these words sound familiar?

The Living Bible says, *"These weapons can break down every proud argument against God **and every wall** that can be built to keep men from finding Him. **With these weapons I can capture rebels and bring them back to God, and change them into men whose heart's desire is obedience to Christ**"* (2 Cor. 10:5 TLB). We're in a spiritual battle to tear down every wall and every stronghold set up in high places to keep mankind away from the knowledge and glory of God.

We're called to rescue rebels and bring them back to God. This is a spiritual battle, and it is only won by God's anointed army using His spiritual word weapons of power. We pray, "Lord, burn this truth deep in our soul, for it's time for us to live in such a way that You can work through us, *'confirming the word with signs following'* (Mark 16:17-20 KJV) and set the captives free!"

> We are called to rescue rebels and bring them back to God

Jesus has given us *"the keys of the kingdom of heaven."* And with these keys we are promised that, **"Whatever you imprison, God will imprison. And whatever you set free,**

God will set free" (Matt. 16:19 NGB). Your mission, should you choose to accept it, is to take up the Lock and Load prophecies of God and demolish the power of wickedness over our land. Set the rebels free and teach them as children of God to obey the love commands of Jesus!

GOD'S MISSION IS TO DESTROY EVERY STRONGHOLD OVER EVERY NATION

As we study these prophecies in detail, we'll see this truth more clearly. The goal of the Lord is to break these demonic strongholds not just over families and cities, but over the nations. A beautiful verse in Amos reveals this truth. It was a time when Israel had turned away from the Lord, and He was calling them to come back to Him: *"The Lord says to the people of Israel, 'Seek Me and live'"* (Amos 5:4 NLV/Rhm). Amos encourages the people, who are prisoners in the enemies' stronghold, *"The Lord is His name. With blinding speed and violence He flashes destruction on the strong,* **breaking all defenses, so that the stronghold is destroyed and laid waste"** (Amos 5:8b-9 NLV/NIV/LB). Seek the Lord. Call upon His name. Let Him *"rain destruction upon the fortresses"* (Phillips). Jesus is *the Stronger One,* and He has come to bind up *the strong man* (satan) and spoil his goods (Luke 11:20-23). God's mission is His Heart of War.

> *With blinding speed and violence the Lord destroys the strongholds*

There's another beautiful way to read Amos 5:8. Many translations read, *"The Lord strengthens those who have been destroyed, spoiled and plundered,* **as He smiles upon them**

they become strong, *and [He will] rain down destruction, spoil and plunder like lightning upon the strongholds"* (DRB/KJV). God desires for all His children from every nation, tribe, race and ethnic group to come unto Him. As He smiles upon us we become strong, and He destroys the strongholds. All of the words of God contain a message of His hope and victory.

Once that spiritual power and stronghold is broken, the people are now free to come home to Him. David rejoiced as God brought him victory over his enemies and said, *"They have lost their courage. They come out of their prison strongholds shaking with fear"* (Psa. 18:45 and 2 Sam. 22:46 NIV/NLV/NET). His enemies are now shaking with holy fear of the Lord. After they come out of their prisons what do they do? They return unto the Lord.

> When God smiles on us, we became strong, we can destroy demonic strongholds

When the nations see the wonders of the Lord, the prophet Micah declares, *"They will come to realize what lowly creatures they really are. Like snakes crawling from their holes, their secret places,* ***their strongholds, they will come out to meet the LORD our God,*** *fill them with holy fear and trembling [as] they stand in awe of Thee"* (Mic. 7:17 NLT/MSG/NET/BBE/MLB). God is at work strengthening us, setting us free, and destroying the strongholds that once held us in captivity. Once we are free, we are able to give God's freedom to the rest of His children.

Under the New Covenant we are called to take up these prophecies and sing them against the evil principalities and powers in high places. Our battle is not against people, we war not against flesh and blood, but against the wicked forces in high places controlling the nations.

The Beautiful Progression of Victory from Isaiah to Daniel

In the next four chapters (3-6) we will study the powerful progression in the four Old Testament Major Prophets. There is a divine progression that flows from Isaiah, to Jeremiah, to Ezekiel, and concludes with Daniel. We will study each of them in detail in the following chapters. All four contain life-changing revelation. As we study these four Major Prophets, we'll notice that the prophecies given by the first three all involve singing.

Here's a brief introduction to God's progression of victory:

1. Isaiah gives us **God's War Songs to tauntingly sing** as we attack our demonic enemies declaring their doom, defeat, and destruction. (See Book One: *The War Songs of God* for an in-depth study.)

2. Jeremiah gives us **God's Lamentations to sarcastically wail** at the *death* of our spiritual adversaries as they die. When they are killed they are cut off and separated from our life.

3. Ezekiel gives us **God's Dirges to mockingly chant** in victory as we *bury* these evil spirits at their funeral and in the name of Jesus put them under our feet forever.

4. Daniel completes this progression with a revelation showing all these **evil forces on the nations are blown away like chaff by the wind of God's Spirit**. Daniel interprets King Nebuchadnezzar's dream and reveals

the kingdoms of this world are replaced by God's Kingdom that will cover the world. For His kingdom is a *"kingdom that will never be destroyed; no one will ever conquer it or be permitted to rule it. It will crush and shatter all these kingdoms into nothingness, but it shall stand forever, indestructible"* (Dan. 2:31-35 and 44-45 NIV/TLB/GW).

After these four prophets, the Minor Prophets jump in and join in the joyful fray of destroying God's enemies. The Lord is taking us somewhere in our faith. We must understand where He is headed so we can be a part of His vital plan of triumph. This is what this book is all about.

The Two Songs Sung in Heaven

The Apostle John tells us that there are two specific songs sung in Heaven before the throne of God. He tells us those who have overcome the evil one are given the harps of God and begin to sing, *"... **the Song of Moses** ... and **the Song of the Lamb**"* (Rev. 15:3). What are these two songs about? They are about the victory we have over the devil, and how we gain this victory by the blood of the Lamb, by the work of Jesus, the Worthy One.

The Song of Moses

What is the song of Moses? There are three songs attributed to Moses in the Old Testament.

They are:

1. The Song of God's Victory over Pharaoh's army (Exodus 15).

2. The Song of Remembrance of the Lord's Covenant to Israel, so they can take the Promised Land (Deut. 31:19 – 32:44).
3. The Song of Prayer asking God to make all they do to succeed (Psalm 90).

All three songs are included in the Song of Moses sung in heaven.

When you combine all of them, you have a song that: 1) declares God's victory over our enemies; 2) reminds us of our Covenant with Him causing us to conquer and possess our promised land, and 3) ends in a prayer we can sing asking God to *"Let Your servants see what You can do for them, let their children see Your glory, let the beautiful favor and graciousness of the Lord our God be upon us, and make all we do succeed and prosper"* (Psa. 90:16-17 JB/DeW/Mof/KJV). As we study *The Lock and Load Prophecies of God*, we shall see that they reflect the three Songs of Moses.

The Song of the Lamb

What is the Song of the Lamb? It is all about the grace, love, mercy, and holiness of Jesus (Rev. 4:8). For He alone is worthy; He alone is worthy to break the seals and break the chains of sin from off of our hearts (Rev. 5:1-6:17). These are songs of God's magnificent grace and love. These songs about Jesus' victory are the visions of hope and triumph included in God's Lock and Load prophecies. Let's work with the Holy Spirit and fulfill Jesus' prayer that just as God's will is being done in heaven; it will also be done on earth (Matt.6:10 & Luke 11:2). One way we will do this is by singing the songs of Moses and the Lamb in the Lock and Load prophecies of God here on the earth.

ENDNOTE

1. Most versions of the Bible do not use the word demon in Psalms 96:5; they use the word idol. The Hebrew word used is *'eliyl* and means "good for nothing, worthless, vain, and empty." It comes from the root word *'al* which means "nothing." Retrieved at: http://www.blbclassic.org/lang/lexicon/lexicon.cfm?Strongs=H457&t=KJV, and http://www.blbclassic.org/lang/lexicon/Lexicon.cfm?Strongs=H408&t=KJV. Nearly all English Bibles translate this verse, "For all the gods of the nations are idols." It is okay to translate this word as worthless demons because both English words agree with the teachings of the Apostle Paul. He tells the church at Corinth that demons and idols are one and the same (See 1 Cor. 10:19-21 NKJV). To God demons are worthless nothings.

CHAPTER THREE

ISAIAH: SING GOD'S TAUNTING WAR SONG

*"You will **take up this taunt-song** against the king of Babylon, and sing, 'How the oppressor has been destroyed! How his tyranny is ended!'"*
—Isaiah 14:4 BBE/NRSV/NET/NLT/CTB

SINGING GOD'S WAR SONGS RELEASES GOD'S GLORY UPON HIS ADVERSARIES

When the Holy Spirit prompts Isaiah to proclaim the Lord's Word against the nations in chapters 13-25, Isaiah delivers fourteen prophetic words against twelve nations calling the prophecies a *"burden from the Lord."* These burdens can also be called War Songs. God also speaks His prophetic burdens, His War Songs through the Minor Prophets: Amos, Nahum, Habakkuk, Zechariah and Malachi.[1] As we sing these prophetic War Songs, we lift up the glory of God and drop His glory upon demonic strongholds crushing them.

The Hebrew word for glory is *kabowd*,[2] and it comes from the root word *kabad*.[3] This root word *kabad* literally means "to be heavy." The best example where we see the effect of the weight of God's glory is when King Solomon dedicated the Temple, *"And it came to pass, when the priests came out of the holy place that the cloud filled the house of the Lord **so that the priests could not stand** to minister because of the cloud; for **the glory of the Lord filled the house of the Lord"*** (1 Kings 8:10-11 NKJV). God's glory is heavy. The weight of the cloud of God's glory literally pressed down on the priests so they could not stand.

In the parallel passage in 2 Chronicles we are told: *"Fire came down from heaven and consumed the burnt offering and the sacrifices and the **Lord's glory** filled the temple. The priests were unable to enter the Lord's temple because **the glory of the Lord had filled the temple**. When all the people saw the fire coming down and the glorious presence of the LORD filling the Temple, **they fell face down on the ground and worshipped and praised the LORD"*** (2 Chron. 7:1-3 NET/NASB/NLT). True worship causes the glory of God to fall on us, and our worship really gets wild when the glory of God falls and fills His house. This is one of the goals of our praise and worship. Oh Lord, fill Your house with Your glory!

This is not just during Old Testament times. The Apostle Paul explains to the church at Corinth that as we prophecy, *"and there come in one who believes not, or one unlearned, he is convicted in his conscience of his sin, and the secrets of his heart are laid bare; **and so falling down on his face he will worship God,** declaring that God is indeed among you"* (1 Cor. 14:24-25

KJV/CV/NEB/Knox). Falling on our face in the presence of the Lord should be a common occurrence in our praise and worship. So our goal in worship is to bless the Lord our God to such a depth that He blesses us with His presence. When the splendor and weight of God's glory falls, we can't stand. All we can do is fall face down on the ground and worship Him.

In the Old Testament the War Songs were sung to lift up the Ark of the Covenant, the Mercy Seat of God (1 Chron. 15:22-28). In the New Testament we sing the War Songs of God to lift up the presence of the Lord Jesus—the new Ark of God's presence. John reveals this truth when he wrote about Jesus and said, *"And the Word became flesh, and* **pitched His tent, did tabernacle among us**" (John 1:14 Rhm/YLT).

As God's glory falls, not only do we fall down on our face, but our demonic oppressors fall down even farther.

> Let the weight of God's glory crush the heads of our enemies

We see that demons must fall before the presence of God when the Ark was captured by the Philistines and they placed it in the temple of their false god, Dagon, *"the next morning, Dagon had fallen with his face to the ground before the Ark of Jehovah!"* (1 Sam. 5: 1-4 TLB). Demons must also fall before the glory of God, and they are underneath us.

The WAR SONGS OF GOD TAUNT his ENEMIES

These prophetic burdens are War Songs that God calls us to sing against His enemies. Over half of them are in the book of Isaiah and are called taunt-songs. God says, *"You shall raise this taunt-song against the king of Babylon* (Isa. 14:4 Mof/CJB). It is imperative that we understand what God means when He commands us to sing a song as a taunt against our spiritual enemies.

What does God mean when He tells us to taunt someone? Webster's 1828 Dictionary (Hardback edition) defines taunt as "to reproach with **severe words**." To reproach means "to censure or rebuke someone deserving disgrace," and it is done "to make their failings more apparent."[4] The word taunt comes from a Persian word that simply means "to pierce with words."[5] This last definition is the key revelation.

> *Our taunts in the Holy Spirit pierce the enemy with the word of GOD*

When we are led by the Holy Ghost to taunt our spiritual enemies, we are piercing them with the Word of God.

As we sing the Word of God, the Word flies through the heavens like fire arrows burning with God's glory. David sang about God's Word being fiery arrows, "*The Lord thundered in the heavens;* **The Most High uttered His voice with hailstones and flames of fire! He shot His arrows** *and scattered His enemies, driving them in all directions; by His flames they were troubled, He vanquished them*" (Psa. 18:13-14 NKJV/DeW/NLT/BBE). Never forget, the devil does not have a shield of faith; he can't stop the flaming missiles of God's Word!

The Burdens, War Songs by Other Prophets

There are other prophets beside Isaiah who proclaim the burden of the Lord, His War Songs. The prophecy given by Nahum is also a *"**burden** of the Lord concerning Nineveh,"* the capital of Assyria (Nah. 1:1 KJV). God comes against these spirits of sorcery and seduction in Assyria which are cruelly oppressing Israel.

Nahum's prophecy is a song with two parts. The Jewish commentators taught that the book of Nahum was composed of two songs.[6] Chapter one is a song about the power of God, and chapters two and three compose a "taunt-song" of God's judgment against Nineveh and their false god belial (Nah. 1:15 JB). Belial, as Paul tells us, is another name for the devil (See 2 Cor. 6:15, compare the KJV with the NLT).

The prophecy of Habakkuk is also a War Song. We are told it is, *"The burden which Habakkuk the prophet did see"* (Hab. 1:1 KJV). It is a War Song against the spirit of violence controlling the nation of Babylon. The Hebrew word used here for violence is *chamac,* but it is pronounced *hamas.*[7] Doesn't that word sound familiar? This spirit is manipulating and motivating Babylon, and this demon of violence is still operating in that same region today.

In the middle of Habakkuk's prophecy we read, *"The time is coming when all their captives [victims of his greed]* **will take up a taunt-song against him, a song of derision***"* (Hab. 2:6a TLB/MLB/Amp). Habakkuk is prophesying of the day that will come when those who have been held prisoner to this spirit of violence will rise up singing the taunt-songs of God against their oppressors.

It is also called a *"song of derision"* (See Berkeley, RSV and Amplified Bible). This is important to note, for we are seated with Jesus in heavenly places (Eph. 2:6), and as God's children, we get to copy what our Father is doing. The Psalms tell us that while the nations rage against the Lord, *"He, Who sits in the heavens is laughing at their threats;* ***the***

Lord shall mock at their madness" (Psa. 2:4 NASB/Knox/Rhm/tPt). When we take our position of authority in Christ, we get to laugh with God against His enemies.

What follows this verse in Habakkuk is a series of five woes we are called to sing with taunts and mocking against that spirit of violence, driving him out of our homes, cities, and nation.[8]

> Sing the wild, enthusiastic, triumphal music of God's war songs of derision

If you don't agree that the whole book of Habakkuk is a song, you have to at least admit that the last chapter is a song for we are told, *"This is a prayer of triumph that Habakkuk **sang** before the Lord"* (Hab. 3:1 TLB). The NASB says to sing this prayer of triumph *"according to Shigionoth,"*[9] which the Amplified Bible describes as ***"wild, enthusiastic, triumphal music."*** This word Shigionoth is used only one other time in the Bible, and that is in the title of Psalm 7.

In this Psalm King David sings for God to *"save and deliver me from all who pursue me,* **or they will tear me like a lion and rip me to pieces** *with no one to rescue"* (vs.1-2 NIV). He cries to God to **"bring to an end the violence of the wicked** *and make the righteous secure"* (vs. 9b NIV). Both times this word Shigionoth is used is in the context of us singing God's victory as He rises up and overthrows the spirit of violence. How we need to *taunt*, to pierce with God's Word, the spirit of violence spreading fear and death over our world!

The last verse of Habakkuk sums it up beautifully, *"The LORD God is my strength and He will make my feet like hinds feet and He will make me to walk upon mine high places* **to the** *chief singer on my stringed instruments"* (Hab. 3:19 KJV). This last verse is loaded with victory! The Hebrew word "to walk" is *darak* and literally means "to march, tread down and trample on."[10] It paints a picture of an army marching in victory over their opponents.

The word for "high places" is *bamah*,[11] and refers to evil high places that nations have erected to worship false gods (See Deut. 12:2, 1 Kings 14:23, 2 Kings 23:8, and Psa. 78:58). So God empowers us like a hind or stag to rise up and walk, to march like an army and tread down the high places where the principalities and powers of evil dwell. Let's discover how the Lord empowers us to do this.

Every Word in the Bible is important. A prime example of this is the short footnote for the musician at the end of Habakkuk's singing prophetic prayer. This footnote tells us how we're empowered by God. Habakkuk ends his singing prophecy with, *"To the chief singer on my stringed instruments"* (Hab. 3:19b KJV). This footnote is comprised of only two words in the Hebrew language, but these two words are so powerful.

Those two words are: *Natsach* and *Negiynah*. These two words are wonderful beyond belief. *Natsach* refers to "an Overcomer with a sonorous voice that leads in music,"[12] and the word *Negiynah* refers to "a taunting or mocking song."[13] The most accurate translation is found in the Septuagint (LXX). It reads, *"The Overcomer leads me in worship; that I may triumph in His taunt-song"* (Hab. 3:19 NETS/CTB). As we follow Jesus, our Chief Singer, He leads us in His War Songs, and we are transformed by His power. We are

> The overcomer leads me in worship that I may triumph in His song

changed into the mighty Stag of the Lord, and as the Army of God we are able to march, to tread down the *"principalities and powers in high places"* who are set against us.

WE DON'T RAIL; WE REBUKE AND REPROACH

As you read about taunting the enemy you may be thinking about the words of warning given in the New Testament by Peter and Jude. They warn us not to give a *"railing accusation"* against the devil. Jude instructs us, *"Even the archangel Michael, when he was disputing with the devil about the body of Moses,* **did not dare to bring a railing accusation** *against him, but said 'The Lord rebuke you!'"* (Jude 1:9 NET/KJV). The archangel Michael did not rail; he rebuked the devil.

Peter uses similar words in his second letter about the wicked: *"especially those who walk after the flesh in the lust of uncleanness, and despise authority. These men are arrogant and presumptuous, they are not afraid to insult celestial beings, rail at dignities, revile the glorious ones. Whereas the angels, which are greater to these in power and might,* **bring not railing accusations against them** *before the Lord"* (2 Pet. 2:10-11 KJV/AAT/Phi/ASV/NEB). Notice that both Jude and Peter use the exact same phrase *"railing accusations."* This warning goes both ways. With Jude it is about men not railing against the devil, a fallen angel, and with Peter, it is used about angels not railing against fallen men.

The word *rail* means "to rant and rage" against someone.[14] It's referring to a person who has lost it emotionally; they are completely out of control. If we fall into the snare of being consumed with anger at the enemy, we become trapped and controlled by our emotions. This same warning and principle apply to physical combat in the natural world. You never want a soldier who has "lost it" to go charging wildly into battle without any control. In a firefight we need our fellow soldiers who are "cool, calm, and collected."

This same principle applies when we fight our spiritual battles; we must be under the control and command of the Holy Spirit, not our emotions. It is not how angry or upset we get at the devil that gives us the victory over him. Our emotions will never defeat the evil one.

Paul warns us, *"Be passionate! But don't let the passion of your emotions lead you to sin!* ***Don't let anger control you or be fuel for revenge,*** *not even for a day.* ***Don't give the slanderous accuser, the devil, an opportunity to manipulate you!"*** (Eph. 4:26-27 tPt). It's the Word, the Name and the Blood of Jesus that causes us to conquer (Rev. 12:11). It is the Lord, not our emotions; who brings His revenge of judgment and victory.

> Our emotions will never defeat the evil one

IT'S HOLY GHOST TAUNTING NOT WORLDLY TAUNTING

So when we attack singing the taunt-songs, the War Songs of God, our taunting is holy and clean. Don't get hung up on the word taunt. Focus on what it means, "to pierce with words." We go forth in victory, *"with the* ***high praises of God*** *in our mouth and* ***a two-edged sword*** *in our hand,* ***for [our] shouted praises are [our] weapons of war!"*** (Psa. 149:6 KJV/tPt). As we sing the Word of God directly against the Lord's adversaries, Jesus, as our Great Overcomer, causes us to tread down the principalities and powers in high places set against us. As we rebuke and "taunt" the enemy, we pierce them with the two-edged sword, the Word of God coming out of our mouth.

When we taunt in the Spirit, we are simply confessing the Word of the Lord. In truth, we proclaim to the enemy, "You lost; Jesus won! You're a loser; the Lord Jesus is the Winner!" It's as simple as that. We just speak the truth, and let the Word of God pierce the evil one.

Remember, the devil and his demons don't have a shield of faith. They cannot quench the fiery word arrows of God's glory as we fire away! With the Word of God we attack, and in the name of Jesus and in the power of His Spirit and by His blood, we conquer them.

The Word of God is a very sharp *"fire-sword, which is full of energy,* **and it pierces more sharply than a soldier's sword"** (Heb. 4:12 tPt and footnote). The Word of God is not a sword when we read it or when we think it. The Word only becomes God's sword when we speak and sing it. And when we speak it, Glory to God, how it pierces the evil one!

> The Word of God becomes the fire-sword of the Lord as we sing it and pierce the evil one

There are more War Songs given by the prophets Amos, Zechariah, and Malachi. The War Songs given by Zechariah and Malachi are covered in detail in *The War Songs of God*. The War Songs by Amos will be covered later in Volume Two of this book.

GOD'S POWER IS RELEASED AS WE SING HIS WAR SONGS

One of the best examples of the power of God's anointing on a song is when David played his harp before King Saul. The unholy spirit of jealousy and murder would depart and leave Saul as *"David would take up his harp and play. Then relief would come to Saul; he would feel better, be refreshed and be well, **and the evil spirit would leave him**"* (1 Sam. 16:23 NET/NASB). When anointed music is played, the power of God's presence falls and demonic spirits must flee or be crushed by the weight of His glory.

Why is singing the Word of God so powerful? Whenever someone preaches, prophecies, prays, or praises the Lord with the Word of God, the Lord anoints His Word that is proclaimed. The anointing on that person is released upon the hearers. What would happen when hundreds, thousands, or tens of thousands of people come together and sing God's Word at the same time? The anointing is magnified a hundred-fold, a thousand-fold as that multitude proclaims the Word of the Lord and sings in unity.

It is the promise the Lord gave to Israel as they fought against their enemies to possess their Promised Land. Joshua told them, *"One of you puts to flight a thousand, since it is the LORD your God Who fights for you, as He promised you"* (Josh. 23:10 NRSV). This was a fulfillment of the promise the Lord had given to them years earlier through Moses to Israel. God through Moses said, *"Five of you will chase a hundred, and a hundred of you will chase ten thousand! All your enemies will fall beneath the blows of your weapons"* (Lev. 26:8 NLT). As more people join in singing God's songs, the force and magnitude of God's glory increases dramatically against the enemy. It's like throwing gasoline on a fire. This huge Holy Ghost explosion is what happens when more of us sing the War Songs of God!

ENDNOTES

1. See Appendix A for a complete list of the War Songs and the first book in "God's Heart of War Series" entitled *The War Songs of God* for an in-depth study.
2. The word *kabowd* at: http://www.blbclassic.org/lang/lexicon/lexicon.cfm?Strongs=H3519&t=KJV.
3. The word *kabad* at: http://www.blbclassic.org/lang/lexicon/Lexicon.cfm?Strongs=H3513&t=KJV.
4. Definition of reproach at: https://www.google.com/?gws_rd=ssl#q=define+reproach.
5. *Noah Webster's 1828 Dictionary* (Hardback Edition).
6. The introduction for Nahum in the *Jewish Study Bible* says his prophecy can be divided into two songs, page 1220.
7. The Hebrew word for violence is *chamac*, but it is pronounced *hamas*. The pronunciation can be heard on the Blue Letter Bible website at: http://www.blbclassic.org/lang/lexicon/lexicon.cfm?Strongs=H2555&t=KJV.
8. See chapters 7-9 in the first book, *The War Songs of God*, for more details.
9. The word *Shigionoth* at: http://www.blbclassic.org/lang/lexicon/lexicon.cfm?Strongs=H7692&t=KJV.
10. The word *darak* at: http://www.blbclassic.org/lang/lexicon/lexicon.cfm?Strongs=H1869&t=KJV.
11. The word *bamah* at: http://www.blbclassic.org/lang/lexicon/lexicon.cfm?Strongs=H1116&t=KJV.
12. The word *Natsach* at: http://www.blbclassic.org/lang/lexicon/lexicon.cfm?Strongs=H5329&t=KJV.
13. The word *Negiynah* at: http://www.blbclassic.org/lang/lexicon/lexicon.cfm?Strongs=H5058&t=KJV.
14. Definition of rail comes from *The American Century Dictionary*.

CHAPTER FOUR

Jeremiah: Wail God's Sacastic Lamentations

*"Babylon is suddenly fallen and destroyed: Howl for her...
Then the heaven and the earth, and **all
that is in them shall sing,**
triumphing over Babylon with joy."*

Jer. 51:8 & 48 KJV/Knox/NAB

Jeremiah, the Sarcastic Prophet of God

The next step in God's progression of victory is found in the lamentations given by the prophet Jeremiah. Bible commentators call him the "weeping prophet"[1] because his book is full of weeping (Hebrew, *nehiy*—"song of wailing or mourning song"[2]) and lamentations (Hebrew, *nehiy*—a "song of wailing or mourning song"[3]). Both words reflect the emotional turmoil we feel when we lament the loss of a close friend or family member.

But before we can study the lamentations of Jeremiah, I must first introduce a radical new revelation of him as a prophet of God. This is a game changer: the lamentations God gave to Jeremiah are to be wailed with *sarcasm*. Yes, you heard me correctly. The Lock and Load prophecies of Jeremiah's lamentations are to be uttered with sarcasm and utter contempt against the evil one.

> God tells us to sing His lamentations with sarcasm

Jeremiah is one of many prophets in the Bible who utilize sarcasm in their prophecies. He, like many of the Old Testament prophets, is very sarcastic when he speaks against demonic, false gods and anyone who follows them. Jeremiah is like the prophet Elijah as he faced the 450 false prophets of Baal and the 400 false prophets of Asherah at Mount Carmel (1 Kings 18:19-20).

Listen as Elijah mocks them and their false gods, *"At midday **Elijah mocked them**: 'Call louder. You'll have to shout louder than that,' **he scoffed**, 'to catch the attention of your god! Perhaps he is talking to someone **or is sitting on the toilet**'"* (1 Kings 18:27 NEB/TLB). Listen how Elijah mocked and scoffed those false prophets—you can hear the sarcasm in his voice. Their god can't answer them; he's too busy sitting on the toilet.

Another prophet who used sarcasm is Nahum. Notice how the Amplified Bible presents Nahum's comments as he is about to address Nineveh and their false god Belial. Nahum says, *"O Judah, keep your solemn feasts, perform your vows: for Belial will never pass through you again: he is utterly cut* *off. [Then **Nahum sarcastically addresses his message to Nineveh**]*" Nah. 1:15b Amp/KJV/JB). This verse introduces the next chapter where Nahum sarcastically warns Nineveh of God's coming judgment. As we can see Jeremiah is not the only prophet who uses godly sarcasm.

BIBLE COMMENTARIES SUPPORT THIS CLAIM OF PROPHETIC SARCASM

This is not a new concept. Perform an internet search of "the sarcasm of Jeremiah" and a quick perusal of a few Bible commentaries will support this claim. Here are a few examples:

1. In Phillip Graham Ryken's book, *Jeremiah and Lamentations: From Sorrow to Hope,* he says, "Many details in Jeremiah's blow-by-blow description of the battle [over Babylon] **were heavy with sarcasm**" in Jer. 50 (p. 689). He adds, "There was **more sarcasm** to come" and gives Jer. 50:21-25 as an example, when Babylon, who is called *"the hammer of the whole earth"* had been pounding away on Israel, will now be *hammered* by God.

2. David A. Peters in his book *The Many Faces of Biblical Humor: A Compendium of the Most Delightful, Romantic, Humorous, Ironic, Sarcastic, or Pathetically Funny Stories and Statements in Scripture* has a whole section on **"Sarcasm and Jeremiah."** He says, "Jeremiah relays **the poignant sarcasm of the Lord."** One example is where God's people *"say unto a stock of wood; You are our father!"* (Jer. 2:26-28 Knox/Sprl). Jeremiah is sarcastically mocking Israel for calling a piece of

wood their god and father. Another is when God asks Israel, *"will you steal, murder, and commit adultery and swear falsely and burn incense unto Baal, and then come here and stand before Me in My temple and chant 'God will save us!' – only to go right back to all these evil things again?"* (Jer. 7:8-11 KJV/TLB). Mr. Peters says, **"The sarcasm of the Lord can be devastating."** He lists many verses as examples. One verse is when Israel has turned her back to God and He proclaims her *freedom*. The Lord says, *"I now proclaim you free, says the Eternal – **free to fall under the sword, the pestilence, and the famine!**"* (Jer. 34:17 Moff). This is when Israel had a hard heart towards God, and is now *free* to experience God's judgement of the sword, pestilence, and famine.

3. Temper Longman in his *Jeremiah, Lamentations (Understand the Bible Commentary Series)* reveals that Jer. 10:1-16 "is reminiscent of the **biting sarcasm** used by Isaiah" in many of his prophecies such as Isa. 40:18-26 and 46:5-13. Notice in all three of these examples the Lord promises eventual victory for Israel, in spite of their rebellion and worship of false gods. How great is the mercy of our God!

4. The NET Bible says the way it translated Jer. 7:18 was, "intended to reflect some of his [Jeremiah's] **ironic sarcasm**." The NET footnote on the verses in Jer. 10:1-5 calls them **"dripping with sarcasm,"** and that the verses in Jer. 23:30-33 "are **filled with biting sarcasm.**"[4]

There are more commentaries that discuss Jeremiah's use of sarcasm,[5] but I believe these four are sufficient enough to support my claim.

Don't misunderstand me. There is genuine weeping, mourning and lamentation when a calamity falls upon an individual or a nation. We see it every day when people die from war and natural disasters, but that's not what God is talking about here. Let's take a closer look at these prophetic words and find out exactly what the Lord is saying through His prophets.

One example is when Jeremiah prophesies against Babylon. He says, "*The whole earth shall shake at Babylon's fall and **her cry of despair shall be heard around the world***" (Jer. 50:46 TLB). This prophecy is repeated in the book of Revelation. We are told when Babylon (the one-world government of the evil one) falls, all the merchants of the world shall cry out with "*weeping and wailing*" (Rev. 18:19 KJV). This is a natural reaction to calamity.

But do we weep as well? No! In the very next verse the Lord commands both heaven and earth to rejoice at the fall of Babylon. God calls His people to, "***Celebrate** over her O Heaven! And People of Christ, and apostles, and prophets **rejoice**!*" (Rev. 18:20 TCNT/Wms). God is not calling to rejoice over any calamity that falls on people, no! He's commanding us to rejoice when a demonic stronghold is destroyed. We don't weep or wail when God's judgment falls on the hosts of hell. We'll never shed one tear when a demon is punished and its stronghold is destroyed by God.

I know you're wondering what in the world am I talking about. And why should we even be concerned about these Old Testament prophecies against ancient nations, many of which no longer exist! Hang in there, and let me explain.

> *We don't weep or wail when God's judgment falls on the hosts of hell*

First, we'll look at God's prophetic Word through Jeremiah (and Ezekiel in the next chapter) against these nations. Then in chapter six, we'll bring it all together and explain why these prophecies are so important today. Here are a few of the wailing lamentations the Lord gives to *"the prophet Jeremiah **against the nations**"* (Jer. 46:1 BBE/JB):

1. Against Egypt he says, *"**The earth is full of your cry and echoes with thy lament**"* (Jer. 46:12 BBE/Knox).
2. Against Philistia he declares, *"The Lord says a flood is coming ... to overthrow the land ... and **the strong men will scream in terror, shriek in alarm and all the land will weep and howl**"* (Jer. 47:2 TLB/KJV/NEB).
3. Against Ammon, he tells the people, *"**Weep and wail**, hiding in the hedges, for your god Milcom shall be exiled along with his princes and priests"* (Jer. 49:3 TLB).
4. Against Babylon he rejoices that *"The whole earth shall shake at Babylon's fall, and **her cry of despair shall be heard around the world**"* (Jer. 50:46 TLB).

All these nations are crying out and wailing their lamentations. Why? If we stopped here, we'd completely miss God's wonderful revelation and the whole reason for these prophecies. A close reading reveals these nations are weeping and wailing because their demons, their false gods have been defeated and driven out by the power of God!

A detailed study shows that these prophetic words are addressed against the false gods, the demonic strongholds ruling over those nations—not against the people] We never pray *against* people; we pray *for* people.

Here are some excellent examples of God's judgment on false gods:

JEREMIAH: WAIL GOD'S SARCASTIC LAMENTATIONS | 59

1. In Egypt the Lord is coming to drive out their false gods. Jeremiah asks them, *"Why has **Apis, your bull god, fled in terror**? Because the Lord knocked him down"* (Jer. 46:15 TLB/Amp). And later he tells them that God comes to judge, *"**Amon** the god of Thebes **and all the other gods**,"* including Pharaoh himself, who was considered a god by the Egyptians (Jer. 46:25 Mof/TLB).

2. In Moab the Lord declares that *"**Chemosh shall go forth into captivity**"* (Jer. 48:7 KJV) and the people of *"Moab shall be **ashamed of Chemosh**"* (Jer. 48:13 KJV)

3. In Ammon the Lord will drive out the demon ruling over them, and their false *"god **Milcom shall be taken prisoner and exiled**"* (Jer. 49:3 TLB/Amp/BBE).

4. And in Babylon when God arrives, their false gods shall fall for *"**Bel shall be confounded** and **Merodach is broken in pieces**; her images are put to shame, **her gods are broken and thrown down**"* (Jer. 50:2 KJV/BBE/Amp). God will *"punish **Bel** the god of Babylon, and pull from his mouth what he has swallowed. **The nations shall no longer come and worship him**; for the wall of Babylon has fallen"* (Jer. 51:44 TLB/RSV) and again he says, the Lord will have a *"**reckoning with those false gods of hers**"* (Jer. 51:52 Knox).

All these names mentioned: Apis, Amon, Chemosh, Milcom, Bel, and Merodach are the names of the false gods, the demonic spirits who have enslaved those nations. A time is coming when God will have a reckoning with them and tear their strongholds down. That time is now!

The world will howl when their false gods fail, we rejoice as a demon is destroyed by God

Hear the words of Jeremiah. He tells us what the heaven and earth will do when demons fall, *"Then the heavens and the earth, and **all that is in them, shall rejoice and sing and shout for joy over Babylon** for the destroyers shall come against them out of the north,' declares the Lord"* (Jer. 51:48 NIV/RSV/CW). These words of Jeremiah's prophecy were fulfilled during the age of the Old Testament when the physical city of Babylon fell at the hands of Darius King of the Medes and Persians (Dan. 5:30-31). But this prophecy has not been completely fulfilled. This word also applies to a more deadly city, a spiritual city that must fall in the last days; it's the stronghold of the antichrist.

In one vision, the angel tells the Apostle John, what he is seeing is *"the Great Whore ...* **MYSTIC BABYLON, THE MOTHER OF HARLOTS AND ABOMINATIONS OF THE EARTH"** (Rev.17:1 &5 Knox/KJV). A day is coming when the Lord will tear down the ultimate demonic stronghold, and oh how we will sing and rejoice!

In the New Testament a divine command is issued from the throne of heaven when spiritual Babylon falls, the Lord God commands us to **"Rejoice over her, O heaven! Rejoice, saints and apostles and prophets!** *For God has judged her for the way she treated you"* (Rev. 18:20 NIV/TLB). The angel of God quotes Jeremiah on purpose. It's time for spiritual Babylon to fall, just as the physical city fell centuries earlier. When a demonic stronghold is destroyed that is the time when the children of God can really rejoice. We don't cry—we have the privilege to sarcastically wail God's lamentations over their Divine destruction.

> *We wail God's lamentations sarcastically because the strongholds He is destroying are demonic*

GODLY SARCASM IS HOLY

Just as the War Songs of God are sung as taunt songs to the enemy (for as we *taunt* them we are in reality "piercing them with God's Word") in the same way, when we are called to sarcastically sing the lamentations of Jeremiah, something powerful happens in the spiritual world. We must understand what God is doing in the Spirit when He tells us to be sarcastic in a godly way.

The word sarcasm literally means "to rip the flesh off."[6] What happens in the spiritual realm when we sing these lamentations with godly sarcasm? When we sing God's Word against these unclean spirits, the Lord tears away that cloak of deception and we clearly see their deeds of darkness such as: sexual perversion, sorcery, deceit, hate, murder, envy, violence, and rage.

The word *flesh* in the Bible represents our old nature and all its evil works. They must be removed from our lives. Paul says we must **"strip off our former way of living,** to cast off our **old nature whose way is destruction**, which yields to deluded passions sinking towards ruin and death; and be renewed in the spirit of your mind; and that you **put on the new nature** of the new life, **which is created to be like God"** (Eph. 4:22-24 Rhm/TCNT/CV/NEB/KJV/Phi/Beck). To walk in victory and live like God, we must strip away our old nature.

Paul gives us a list of the works of the flesh that must be cast off: *"Now the works of the flesh are quite obvious, such as adultery, fornication, impurity, sensuality, idolatry, witchcraft (or sorcery), hatred, strife, jealousy, passionate anger, fits of rage ... murder, drunkenness and such like"* (Gal. 5:19-21 KJV/Mof/CV/NEB). Notice that even witchcraft or sorcery is called a work of the flesh. We must rid our life of these behaviors of our old nature because *"those controlled by the flesh cannot please God"* (Rom. 8:8 Rhm/KJV). So we get to "sarcastically wail" as the wicked deeds of poor, miserable Milcom are exposed and destroyed, as the cruel work of big bad Bel is broken and the violence of mean Merodach is driven away. In the spiritual realm, as we sing God's Word with God's sarcasm, the Lord *kills* that demon as He *separates* us from it and the works of our flesh. I will explain this in more detail in a minute

It is the demonic spirits ruling in high places that the Lord has called us to proclaim His Word against and pull down. Jesus says that their leader, satan, the prince of the power of the air must *"fall like lightning"* when the Word of God is preached (Luke 10:18 NEB). Demons are not stronger than their leader, if satan must fall at the preaching of the Gospel, they must fall as well!

> The work of Godly sarcasm is to remove the flesh from our lives

This is the power contained in the Word of God, and salvation is found in no other name than the name of Jesus (Acts 4:12). At the name of Jesus every knee shall bow and every tongue confess that Jesus is Lord (Rom. 14:11). That means a day is coming when satan and all the host of hell will bow their knee and confess with their mouth that Jesus is Lord, for *"all who dwell in heaven, and in earth,* **and those in the demonic realm will confess that Jesus Christ is Lord to the glory of God the Father"** (Phil. 2:10 KJV/Wey/tPt). Every tongue means every tongue; not one is exempt.

GOD'S DESTINY IS PEACE FOR EVERY NATION

The purpose of all of God's judgments is not to just bring correction and deliverance into our lives but, to bring us into a future full of hope. The Lord says, *"'I have not lost sight of My plan for you,' the Lord says, 'and it is your welfare I have in mind, not your undoing; I will help you, not hurt you; for you too, I have a destiny of peace and a future full of hope for you'"* (Jer. 29:11 Knox/JB/CW). The Lord's plan is a destiny full of peace and hope for all of His children, no matter whom they have worshipped and served. For most of these nations the Lord ends His Lock and Load prophecy with a message of restoration, mercy, and a vision of hope for the people of that nation who repent and come to the Lord.

> God's destiny of peace: "I will help you, not hurt you"

God's purpose and goal for every country is one of glorious restoration. For each nation the Lord includes His glorious conclusion. Read out loud His vision of victory for them:

1. For Israel – *"**I will not destroy you.** I will punish you as you deserve, **but only enough to correct you**"* (Jer. 46:28b TLB/NEB).

2. For Moab – *"'But in the latter days,' says the Lord, **her lot will be reversed, I will establish and restore the fortunes of Moab, and she will prosper again**'"* (Jer. 48:47 TLB/NIV/Knox/CW).

3. For Ammon – *"But afterwards **I will change the fate of the children of Ammon; I will bless Ammon and she will prosper again; I will restore the fortunes of the Ammonites and bring the exiled sons of Ammon back to their home"*** (Jer. 49:6 RSV/BBE/NAB/Knox/CW).

4. For Elam – *"'But in the latter days **I will bring the people back, I will reverse the fate and captivity of Elam, I will restore the fortunes of Elam, and once again she will prosper, and I bring them back to their home' says the Lord"*** (Jer. 49:39 TLB/NIV/Knox/BBE/CW).

This is God's Heart of War in action. He goes into battle to set all of His children free, whoever they are. The Lord Jesus goes forth as the Divine Warrior restoring them into His family of grace and mercy. We have the honor to be used by Him in this glorious warfare to rescue and restore.

SARCASTICALLY WAIL GOD'S LAMENTATION WHEN A DEMON DIES

When Jeremiah releases the Lock and Load prophecies of God in chapters 46-51, he releases the roar of the Lord against the nine nations of Egypt, Philistia, Moab, Ammon, Edom, Syria, Elam, Arabia, and Babylon. Jeremiah does not proclaim burdens or war songs like Isaiah, but specific prophecies called wailing lamentations. Why?

Just as the physical world has lamentations they wail when destruction falls, we have songs in the Spirit we sing when demonic principalities and powers have been attacked and destroyed by God. The War Songs of God are just that; they are songs that call us into war. But once the battle is over there is no need for a War Song. Once our adversary is dead, it's time to sing the Lord's lamentations and sarcastically mourn their *death*.

Throughout the Bible when a city or nation was destroyed, the other nations would either rejoice or mourn at their demise depending on whether they were enemies or allies with the nation being destroyed. Lamentations are used in this respect throughout the book of Jeremiah, but we need to see the mystery of these lamentations in the spiritual realm.

Many stories in the Old Testament are physical examples of what goes on in the spiritual world. Paul explains in 1 Corinthians that the events we read about in the Old Testament which happened to Israel *"are examples to us, warning us—lessons that teach us not to fail in the same way by callously craving worthless things and practicing idolatry, as some of them did"* (1 Cor. 10:6-7a KJV/Nor/tPt). We take these events *"that provide us with a warning so that we can learn through what they experienced. For we live in a time when the purpose of all the ages is now completing its goal within us"* (1 Cor. 10:11b tPt). We learn what to do and what not to do as we walk with the Lord.

All the battles in the natural realm given in the Old Testament are examples of how we are to do battle with our demonic opponents today in spiritual warfare. In the holy war God has called us to do battle in, we not only attack demonic forces; God has called us to kill them.

God has called us to not just attack demonic forces; He commands us to kill them

SO HOW DO WE KILL A DEMON?

You're probably asking, "How in the world do we kill a demon?" Before I can answer how we do this, I need to first ask you; what is a good one-word definition for death? When I asked this question to my son Seth, he came up with two excellent words. He immediately answered "silenced and immobilized." Good answer, something that is dead no longer talks and walks. A dead devil can no longer chase us and hit us with his words of accusation. But there is another good one-word Biblical definition for death; it's the word *separated*.

Remember the story of Adam and Eve in the Garden of Eden? God warned Adam if he ate of the fruit of the Tree of Knowledge of Good and Evil, *"in the day that you eat from it you shall surely die"* (Gen. 2:17 NKJV). When Adam and Eve rebelled and ate of the fruit of the Tree of Knowledge, they were cast out of Eden and *separated* from God. They did not die physically that day, but the second they sinned, they were *separated* from the presence of God.

That day they died spiritually.

It was 930 years later when Adam's spirit *separated* from his body; he died physically (Gen. 5:5). Since a thousand years is as a day to the Lord (2 Pet. 3:8), Adam did not live a full day before God. Another example of how the word separated means death is that, even today, when a couple is *separated* due to hurts or unfaithfulness; we say their relationship has *died*.

When Jesus cast out a demon, He causes that spirit to leave, to be separated from that person's life. When we walk in God's presence and speak His powerful Word against spiritual powers they are cut off, they are *separated* from us and our family. They are as good as dead to us as far as their influence on our life and our home is concerned. Also their lies are *silenced* and they no longer buffet us because they have become *immobilized* by the power and grace of God. As far as we're concerned, they are *dead* to us.

When a demon is cast out of our life, it is now dead to us, and we have the honor to sarcastically wail a lamentation over their death. Don't get hung up on the word sarcasm. Instead grab hold of what the Lord is doing, His revelation behind the word. Just as we don't focus on taunting the evil one, we focus on what it means. We get to "pierce him with the Word" of God. So our purpose is not so much to be sarcastic, but to sing the lamentations of God so the flesh is cut away, the old nature is separated from us. It is killed by the power of Jesus and dead as far as our life is concerned.

> When demons are cast out, they're dead to us— separated from us

There is one slight problem; demonic spirits don't want to remain *dead*. Jesus warns us that once an evil spirit is cast out of a person, it returns *"and brings seven other spirits more evil than itself, and they go in and live there, so the last state of that person is worse than the first"* (Luke 11:26 NET). Thank God, He has given us a solution for this problem! In the next chapter we will discover God's guidance to secure our permanent victory over spiritual forces. A further step in God's path of triumph is found in the mocking dirges of Ezekiel.

ENDNOTES

1. Jeremiah is called "the weeping prophet" at: https://en.wikipedia.org/wiki/Jeremiah.
2. The word *caphad* at: http://www.blbclassic.org/lang/lexicon/lexicon.cfm?strongs=H5594&t=KJV.
3. The word *nehiy* at: http://www.blbclassic.org/lang/lexicon/lexicon.cfm?Strongs=H5092&t=KJV.
4. Here are the references for the Bible Commentaries concerning the sarcasm that Jeremiah used in his prophecies:
   a. Phillip Graham Ryken's *Jeremiah and Lamentations: From Sorrow to Hope*, At: https://books.google.com/books?id=SxwunnpoBggC&pg=PA395&lpg=PA395&dq=the+sarcasm+of+Jeremiah&source=bl&ots=8u5k9dxJlt&sig=zv3diHUG1ov1PZ7o38kI6nN6tQ0&hl=en&sa=X&ei=-TuQVMnzBM6cyASFioCgDA&ved=0CCQQ6AEwAQ#v=onepage&q=the%20sarcasm%20of%20Jeremiah&f=false.
   b. David A. Peters *The Many Faces of Biblical Humor: A Compendium of the Most Delightful, Romantic, Humorous, Ironic, Sarcastic, or Pathetically Funny Stories and Statements in Scripture*. At: https://books.google.com/books?id=Dpm4Rnx97bQC&pg=PA205&lpg=PA205&dq=the+sarcasm+of+Jeremiah&source=bl&ots=mV3cnUqcPD&sig=hivIUh0ervei4cHitj9sAc7du4s&hl=en&sa=X&ei=-TuQVMnzBM6cyASFioCgDA&ved=0CDQQ6AEwBA#v=onepage&q=the%20sarcasm%20of%20Jeremiah&f=false.
   c. Temper Longman *Jeremiah, Lamentations (Understand the Bible Commentary Series)*https://books.google.com/books?id=wDlXoM_zW64C&pg=PT143&lpg=PT143&dq=the+sarcasm+of+Jeremiah&source=bl&ots=e94oKcCw4E&sig=tjxPcmQN00Tu29SQmHnAEXnXz8o&hl=en&sa=X&ei=-TuQVMnzBM6cyASFioCgDA-&ved=0CDoQ6AEwBg#v=onepage&q=the%20sarcasm%20of%20Jeremiah&f=false. The NET Bible footnotes to Jer. 10:1-5 and 23:30-33.
5. A few more commentaries that mention Jeremiah's use of sarcasm are:
   a. *Ellicott's Commentary* says there is **"a touch of sarcasm"** in Jer. 8:22, at: http://biblehub.com/commentaries/jeremiah/46-11.htm.
   b. Dr. Henry Morris of the Institute for Creation Research justifies Jeremiah's **"occasional touch of sarcasm"** like he uses in Jer. 2:27-28 is warranted at times. At: http://www.icr.org/article/5632/.
   c. The editors of Troubling Jeremiah list many verses which they say are examples where, "Jeremiah uses sarcasm to attribute ridiculous claims to the people" who worship idols. At: https://books.google.com/books?id=PmOvAwAAQBAJ&pg=PA254&lpg=PA254&dq=the+sarcasm+of+Jeremiah&source=bl&ots=riIdHRrEHb&sig=8U-X-HFhjatyNVYsODORNN_j01c&hl=en&sa=X&ei=-TuQVMnzBM6cyASFioCgDA&ved=0CD0Q6AEwBw#v=onepage&q=the%20sarcasm%20of%20Jeremiah&f=false
6. The definition of sarcasm from the Merriam-Webster Dictionary at: http://www.wordcentral.com/cgi-bin/student?va=sarcasm.

CHAPTER FIVE

EZEKIEL: CHANT GOD'S MOCKING DIRGES

*Son of Man, **sing a funeral song** [a dirge] over the king of Tyre.*

Ezek. 28:12a NET/MSG/EXB

EZEKIEL CHANTS DIRGES NOT LAMENTATIONS

When demonic influences are cast out of our life, Jesus says they return and attempt to re-enter their old *home* (Luke 11:24-26). What is God's solution to this problem? We find His victorious answer in the dirges of the prophet Ezekiel.

Like Jeremiah, Ezekiel also cries out to the Lord due to the sins and bondage of Israel. But with Ezekiel, the Holy Spirit does not have the prophet sing War Songs (like

Isaiah), nor does He have him decree wailing lamentations (like Jeremiah). Instead the Lord has Ezekiel chant *dirges*—funeral songs—over the false gods of the nations who are attacking His people.

Some Bible translations including the King James Version, the New International Version, and the New American Standard Bible cause confusion concerning the dirges of Ezekiel. This confusion arises because they use the same English word "lamentation" in Ezekiel as was used for Jeremiah's prophetic words. It makes the reader believe that both Ezekiel and Jeremiah are proclaiming lamentations for the Lord. This is not correct.

Jeremiah and Ezekiel use totally different Hebrew words in their prophecies. As mentioned in the last chapter, Jeremiah uses two Hebrew words, *nehiy* and *caphad*, that are correctly translated *lamentations*. Remember, the first word refers to a "wailing, mourning song," and the second word means "to wail, lament, and mourn." But Ezekiel uses two totally different Hebrew words when he prophesies. The words he uses are *qiynah* and *quwn,* which refer to a different kind of mourning, a specific type of wailing.

The word *qiynah* does refer to a lamentation but it's a specific type called a "dirge or elegy."[1] It comes from the Hebrew root word *quwn* which means "to chant a dirge or to sing a mourning song."[2] A dirge is an elegy. Don't confuse an elegy with a eulogy. A eulogy is "a speech in praise of a person, especially an oration in honor of someone who has died."[3] The prophetic words of Ezekiel are definitely not eulogies! They

> *We chant the dirges of the Lord as God buries our adversaries under our feet*

don't praise a demon when it dies. No, they are elegies: "mournful, melancholy, or plaintive poems, especially a funeral song or lament."[4] Most modern translations like the NLT, NCV, MSG, Voice, the GNT and other versions translate *qiynah* accurately as a *"funeral song"* or *"dirge."* The prophecies of Ezekiel give us dirges or funeral songs to sing, because after we attack and kill our demonic adversaries, we must then *bury* them under our feet by the power of our God.

The Mocking Dirges, the Funeral Songs of Ezekiel

Just like Jeremiah, there is something added to Ezekiel's dirges. The special elements added to his prophetic words are attitudes of *scorn* and *mockery*.

Here's an enlightening passage from a study on Ezekiel by Ronald M. Hals concerning the dirges of Ezekiel. Mr. Hals says, "The dirge belongs properly to the setting of a funeral," but when Ezekiel adds "an element of political **mockery** ... then of course **grief is replaced by scorn**" (emphasis mine).[5] The dirges of Ezekiel are not dirges of grief; they are dirges of mockery, scorn, and derision against our spiritual enemies. As we study the dirges of Ezekiel, we'll understand this amazing revelation and change our perception of these dirges.

Mr. Hals makes a vital observation concerning Ezekiel's dirges for the city of Tyre (Ezek. 26 -28). He says when the prophets employ a dirge they were taking "an even bigger step, usually **involving scorn and mockery, and giving the feeling of power because they treat their subject as being as good as dead**. The then-now contrast often lent itself to

this dimension of derision of the once mighty" (emphasis mine).[6] Do you catch what Mr. Hals said? Ezekiel employs *scorn and mockery* in his dirges *giving the feeling of power to* Israel because her demonic adversaries are *as good as dead* to them! The idea our enemy is dead to us is not a new idea; Hals wrote his commentary nearly thirty years ago.

Hals notes that Ezekiel's dirge over Tyre would "come to **serve as a model** for some of the sections in Revelation 18, especially vv. 1-8, which ... **appear in a context of the most intense hostility**" (emphasis mine). He goes on to say that dirges were used by prophets to denounce their enemies. The dirge or funeral song of the prophet is focused "on the hubris of the enemy, who flaunts divine sovereignty."[7] Hubris denotes conceit, extreme arrogance, and foolish pride. Yes, it is very foolish to defy God.

Notice all the words I highlighted in this lengthy quote: "scorn and mockery," their enemy is "treated as being as good as dead." In the dirge there is a "feeling of power" and a "dimension of derision" with "intense hostility" against our enemy. One last comment made by Hals is that while the dirge is sung; we must understand that these words are "Yahweh's own word(s)."[8] All of these attitudes are involved when we dance and sing the dirges of the Lord as we address our spiritual enemy in our warfare worship. We're singing "Yahweh's own words" against our adversaries which intensifies the victory we have over them.

> *The dirges of God give us His power and His attitude of derision against our enemies because in in Jesus, they are as good as dead to us*

The Scorn, Satire, and Sarcasm of Ezekiel

Here are some examples of Bible commentaries that show Ezekiel, like Jeremiah, is a prophet who uses sarcasm and satire in his prophetic judgements against God's enemies:

1. In James E. Smith's *Ezekiel: A Christian Interpretation*, he has a section entitled "Ezekiel 13 Scathing Oracles" and says, "**Surely it must have been with sarcasm** that Ezekiel referred to his opponents as *the prophets of Israel*" (p.161). And on his commentary on Ezekiel 19:1-9 which he entitles a "Dirge over Judah's Kings" he says, "With **biting sarcasm** the prophet refers to these young rulers as powerful young lions" (p. 214).

2. The writer of the *Grace thru Faith* website says that the Lord's comment through Ezekiel "to the human ruler of Tyre **was heavy on the sarcasm**, implying he thought he was wiser than Daniel because of the success he enjoyed, even considering himself to be a god" (Ezekiel 28:1-5). The Lord proved the king of Tyre was not wise but very stupid.

3. In *A Complete Literary Guide to the Bible* edited by Ryken and Longman there is a section about Old Testament prophecy written by Richard Patterson and which notes that the book of "**Ezekiel includes satire in its laments [i.e. Dirges].**"

4. The *ESV Study Bible* has a section on Ezekiel's oracles of judgment and says they "are ordinarily examples of satire and in **the prophetic satire of Ezekiel** there are three motifs: (1) description of

evil, (2) denunciation of this evil, and (3) warnings and predictions that God will judge the evil."[9]

There are more commentaries about Ezekiel's "biting sarcasm,"[10] but these four should be enough proof that this is not a crazy, obscure idea.

Notice the last two commentaries indicate that Ezekiel is using satire in his dirges against evil. Satire is a synonym for sarcasm and means to use "humor, irony, or ridicule to expose and criticize people's stupidity or vices."[11] From the word ridicule, we get the word ridiculous which means to laugh. Remember that the Lord laughs at the ridiculous and feeble threats of His enemies. In Psalm 2 we read, *"He Who sits in heaven is laughing at their threats, **amused at all their puny plans, the LORD mocks their madness**"* Psa. 2:4 KJV/Knox/tPt). If God is laughing at the *threats and puny plans* of His enemies; then we need to be laughing at their *madness* as well.

> When God laughs, all of heaven resounds with His joy and mirth

We can only laugh at the evil one if we are seated with Jesus in the heavenlies. From this position, we see things correctly. We see things how God sees them. God only has visions of victory. The Apostle Paul promises us that *"even though our sins had made dead men of us, God has made us ... live again and share the life of Christ, (by grace you were saved) and has raised us up together with Him from the dead, and **enthroned us to sit with Him in heavenly places**"* (Eph. 2:5-6 KJV/Knox/AAT/CV/Wey). It is only here, in this place of authority, sitting with Jesus in the heavenly realms that we may laugh with the Father at the enemy.

The higher we ascend into the throne room of God and the closer we come into His presence, the more we will laugh at the evil one. Don't you know that when the Father God begins to laugh, that all the mountains and trees of creation are ringing with the sounds of His joy. God's throne room is filled with laughter against the threats of our spiritual enemies.

The Dirges of Ezekiel

The Lock and Load prophecies of Ezekiel are given in the form of dirges. They come against the nations: Ammon, Moab, Edom, Philistia, Tyre, Sidon, Egypt, Ethiopia, Assyria, Elam, Meshech, and Tubal (Ezek. 25-39). Though many of these nations no longer exist; the spiritual strongholds still reside in these regions. Here are a few examples of where God gives Ezekiel a dirge to chant.

Against Tyre the Lord says,

> "Now, son of man, take up a lamentation, **a dirge against Tyre**" (Ezek. 27:2 KJV/AAT), and "Son of man, **sing a dirge, rise up a funeral song** against the king of Tyre"(Ezek. 28:12 NET/AAT/MSG).

And later against Egypt the Lord says.

> "This is a dirge; they will chant it, and **the women will sing it as a dirge … Chant it as a dirge** over Egypt for the death of its pomp. **Chant it over all its horde.** I, the Sovereign LORD have spoken!"(Ezek. 32:16 NEB/NET/MSG/NLT/NRSV).

Just like the lamentations of Jeremiah, these dirges of Ezekiel are songs of sarcasm. The Lord has spoken! We are called to chant them, mocking the hordes of the evil one.

A WORD OF CAUTION

A word of instruction and caution is needed here. In Isaiah and other prophets, we are called to sing the War Songs as taunt songs against the enemy. As we noted earlier, the word taunt simply means to "pierce with words," so we pierce the evil one with the word of God in our praise and worship. Then with Jeremiah we are to sing the wailing lamentations sarcastically. The word sarcasm means "to rip the flesh off." As we wail the Lord's lamentations the work of the flesh and the deeds of darkness are cut away from our lives and the lives of others by God (Rom. 8:8). Now God calls us to mockingly chant the dirges of Ezekiel at our adversaries' funeral.

The definition of the word mock is "to laugh in a scornful manner with no intention to deceive."[12] When we mock the evil one, we never do it the world's way. We must mock God's way with no deception in it, just the truth.

HOW DO WE MOCK LIKE GOD?

Let's look at three different Hebrew words for mock in the Old Testament to understand clearly why the Lord calls us to chant His dirges with mockery. The first word is *hathal* and means "to mock," but it also means "to cause to fall!"[13] It can literally mean "to reveal the teachings of the covenant and the Cross."[14] As the teaching of God's covenant in the Cross of Jesus is revealed, it causes the evil one to fall like lightning (Luke 10:17-19).

The second word is *sachaq* and means "to laugh usually in contempt, to mock, and to play including music, singing and dancing."[15] One possible literal meaning is "to destroy the stronghold that tries to hold back our destiny."[16] As we sing and dance before the Lord, the stronghold of the enemy trying to hold back our destiny is destroyed.

The third word is the Hebrew root word *la ag* and means "to mock, deride, and ridicule," but mainly it means "to stammer!"[17] A derivative from this word is *la'eg* which means "to stammer and mock."[18] This derivative word, *la'eg,* is used by Isaiah when he promises that the Lord will come and "*with* **mocking, stammering lips and another tongue** *He will speak to this people*" (Isa. 28:11 NET/KJV). Paul quotes this verse from Isaiah to reveal the promise of God is fulfilled when He gives us the gift of speaking in tongues (1 Cor. 14:21-22). Paul says, "*So then, tongues are not a sign for believers,* **but a miracle for unbelievers**" (1 Cor. 14:22a tPt). As we speak in tongues, it's a miracle for unbelievers because it's a weapon we use to resist the evil one. Speaking in tongues is one of God's holy ways for us to mock our enemy!

> God mocks the demonic strongholds that try to hold back our destiny

Putting all three of these Hebrew words together we understand the Lord's command on how we mock the hosts of darkness in His divine way. When we mockingly chant His dirges in our praise and worship, we release *the teachings of the covenant of the Cross* which *cause* the evil ones *to fall.* Our *playing, singing, and dancing* in worship sounds like funeral songs, dirges to the devil; as we *destroy the stronghold*

> *In the spiritual realm to the devils' ears, singing in tongues sounds like a mocking funeral dirge*

trying to hold back our destiny. And as we "sing rapturous praises in the Spirit [in tongues]" (1 Cor. 14:15 NET/KJV/tPt), it is a mocking funeral song in the ears of the hosts of hell! As we chant the Dirges of God we break those strongholds that have held back our destiny. As we chant, we soar up into the heavenlies; we cause the enemy to fall. All that's left for us to do is laugh with God, as He laughs at them.

CAN YOU BURY A DEMON?

It is not good enough for demons to be cast out, separated, and killed as far as their influence over our lives are concerned. Remember how Jesus warned us and said when a demon is cast out or separated from us it will try to come back into our life. Jesus said, *"When an evil spirit goes out of a person, it travels over dry country looking for a place of rest. If it can't find one, it says to itself,* **'I will go back to my house'"** (Luke 11:24 GNB). It is not enough to separate that demon from our life and the lives of others. It's not good enough to *kill* a demon, because they try to come back home. We don't leave demonic corpses floating around. They need to be buried.

So how do we bury a demon? We find that answer in God's lovely words to Nahum. Through the prophet Nahum, the Lord declares to Belial, the worthless one, which is another name for the devil, *"The Lord has given an order about you* [God is talking to the wicked counselor of verse 11]; *the Lord has issued a command concerning you. Your name shall be perpetuated no longer; out of the house of your gods I will cut off the carved Image; I will destroy your gods and temples.* **I will dig your grave and I will bury you,** *for you are vile and stink with sin"* (Nah. 1:14 JUB/BBE/NASB/NRSV/NKJV/TLB). Glory to God!

Some translations have God speaking this command to Assyria or its capital Nineveh, but this is not correct. There is no word in the Hebrew text here for Nineveh or Assyria. The Lord's command is against Belial, the wicked counselor, mentioned earlier in verse 11, who is operating through the leaders of Assyria: *"From you, Nineveh, there is one come full of wicked schemes, who plotted against the Lord, a* **counsellor of Belial**" (Nah. 1:11 HCSB/JUB/KJV). This word is not against Nineveh or Assyria but against Belial. Look at the next verse for conformation of this claim.

The Lord continues to proclaim through Nahum, *"Look, there on the mountains,* **the feet of the one who proclaims good news of peace! 'No more worries about this enemy, he has been wiped out and we are safe!'** *Celebrate your festivals, O Judah, and fulfill your vows to worship the Lord only, for* **Belial will never pass through you again; he has been cut off forever, utterly destroyed; he will never be seen again"** (Nah. 1:15 NIV/NJB/TLB/MSG).

God is promising us that *"Belial will never pass through you and attack you again; he has been cut off forever, utterly destroyed; he will never be seen again"* (ERV/JB). We won't see him again because God has buried him under our feet. You know when the LORD digs a grave; a grave has truly been dug, and that demon called Belial is going down! No longer will he oppress us. When God buries a

> When God digs a grave it's dug—and the demon Belial is going down!

demon, that spirit is buried for good and can never return to harass us.

At the end of this verse the Amplified Bible adds an interesting line as an introduction to the next chapter as Nahum predicts the fall of Nineveh. It reads, *"Then the prophet Nahum **sarcastically** addresses his message to Nineveh."* God is not finished with His sarcasm against His enemies; He has only just begun. If we read the next two chapters of Nahum, we'll see they are a taunting War Song of victory over Belial who's been ruling over Nineveh.

GOD'S HOLY GHOST BURIAL CREW

That's not all, there is more! Who gets to be God's gravediggers? Who gets to be a part of God's Holy Ghost burial crew? We do! This promise of victory in the good news of the Gospel was first given by Isaiah. He proclaims, *"How beautiful on the mountains are the feet of those who bring good news, who proclaim peace,* **who brings good news of happiness, who announces salvation, and says to Zion, 'Your God reigns!'"** (Isa. 52:7 NIV/NASB). Paul echoes Isaiah's words and tells us this verse is referring to the good news of the Gospel of Jesus (Rom. 10:15). Anyone preaching the Gospel of Jesus gets to be God's gravedigger, we get to be a part of His Holy Ghost burial crew! Glory to God, everybody grab a shovel!

> *Everybody grab a shovel, preach the Good News and see demons put under our feet as God buries them*

The disciples rejoiced when they returned from preaching the Gospel, *"they were ecstatic with joy"* and declared to Jesus, *"Lord, even the demons obey us when we speak in*

Your name" (Luke 10:17 NIrV/tPt). As we preach the Gospel satan and the demons fall under our feet. Once these spirits are "buried" we walk over their graves. They are literally and totally under our feet.

The beautiful Words of Jesus are fulfilled: *"Jesus said, 'I saw satan fall like lightning from heaven.* **I have given you the authority to advance, to tread and trample on serpents and scorpions, safe passage as you walk among snakes and scorpions and crush them,** *over* **all** *the power of the enemy and* **protection from every assault of the enemy, and nothing shall by any means hurt you.** *You will trample upon every demon before you and overcome every power satan possesses. Nevertheless, do not rejoice in this, that spirits submit to you, but rejoice that your names are written in heaven. This is the true source of your authority'"* (Luke 10:19-20 NKJV/NLT/Wuest/MSG/NRSV/tPt). In Jesus, as we march, He gives us *"safe passage as you walk on snakes and scorpions and crush them."* You have Jesus' authority to *trample upon every demon before you and overcome every power satan possesses.* 'But the best news is not that evil spirits obey us, but that our names are recorded in heaven.

Jesus says, *"The great triumph is not in your authority over evil, but in God's authority over you and (His) presence with you.* **Not what you do for God but what God does for you**—*that's the agenda for rejoicing"* (MSG). By the power of the Gospel the enemy was placed under the disciple's feet. They could safely walk over and crush snakes and scorpions because they're buried by God, but best of all, their names are recorded in heaven.

> Jesus has given us the command to march, crushing spiritual forces as we rejoice

The powerful promise Paul gave to the believers in the Church at Rome comes alive in our life, *"**The God of peace will soon crush satan under your feet.** Enjoy the best of Jesus!"* (Rom. 16:20 NJB/MSG). There is no greater peace than when God crushes the head of satan under our feet. If we are not experiencing the peace of the Lord in a certain area in our life that is a sure sign that there's a problem or harassment that's not under our feet.

There is no greater peace than walking on the devil's head

Ask Jesus to give you the victory in that area, so we can all enjoy the best of Jesus in His peace and victory!

Let me give a practical example in my life of a demon that is dead and buried. For me it's the demon of sorcery or witchcraft. The Greek word is *pharmakeia* and means using drugs for witchcraft and sorcery.[19] By the grace of God I have never been tempted to take drugs or get involved with sorcery or witchcraft. That demonic influence has been killed and is buried under my feet. There may be other areas in my life that I am working out the victory by the blood and name of Jesus, but for me, by the grace of God, that demon of *pharmakeia* is dead and buried.

GOD'S WORK IN OUR LIVES IS TO MAKE US LIKE JESUS

The heart of God is for all His sons and daughters to be like Jesus. As Jesus prepared to go to the Cross He told the disciples, *"The prince of this godless world is coming and about to attack. But don't worry **he has nothing in Me that belongs to him**; he has no claim on Me and **he has no power over Me**"*

(John 14:30 NIV/MSG/AMP). This is God's life goal for all of us. For us to come to a place in our lives where there is nothing of the devil in us, and as a result he has no power over us. But that is not all.

What does Jesus say next? He says, *"I will freely do exactly what the Father requires of Me so that the world will know that I love the Father"* (John 14:31 TLB/NCV). Because the evil one has nothing in us, no power over us; we are now free to do exactly what the Father wants us to do in this life. And the world will know that we love the Father. Hallelujah! To summarize:

- ISAIAH—we tauntingly sing war songs as demons are defeated.
- JEREMIAH—we sarcastically wail God's lamentations as demons die.
- EZEKIEL—we mockingly chant God's dirges as God buries them.

ENDNOTES

1. The word *qiynah* at: http://www.blbclassic.org/lang/lexicon/lexicon.cfm?Strongs=H7015&t=KJV.
2. The root word *quwn* at: http://www.blbclassic.org/lang/lexicon/Lexicon.cfm?Strongs=H6969&t=KJV.
3. Definition of a eulogy at: http://dictionary.reference.com/browse/eulogy.
4. Definition of an elegy at: http://dictionary.reference.com/browse/elegy.
5. *Ezekiel, The Forms of the Old Testament Literature, Volume XIX*, Ronald M. Hals, (Grand Rapids, William B. Eerdmans: 1989), page 130.
6. Ibid, page 194.
7. Ibid.
8. Ibid, page 187.
9. Here are the references for the quotes on sarcasm and satire in Ezekiel:
    a. In James E. Smith's *Ezekiel: A Christian Interpretation*, At: https://books.google.com/books?id=jwwXAgAAQBAJ&pg=PA161&lpg=PA161&dq=sarcasm+in+Ezekiel&source=bl&ots=ODPbnUALfq&sig=lzI3Pbx8S9HcZTIuS9Xt1uOgy80&hl=en&sa=X&ei=7DGUVLjaL8mngwToxIPIDQ&ved=0CCsQ6AEwAg#v=onepage&q=sarcasm%20in%20Ezekiel&f=false.
    b. The writers of the Grace thru Faith website, at: http://gracethrufaith.com/ask-a-bible-teacher/ezekiel-know-daniel/.
    c. *A Complete Literary Guide to the Bible* ed. Ryken and Longman. http://christandpopculture.com/mock/.
    d. The *ESV Study Bible* has a section on Ezekiel's oracles of judgment at: http://esvstudybible.org/wp-content/uploads/excerpt-ezekiel-intro.pdf.
10. Here are two more examples of sarcasm in the book of Ezekiel:
    a. In Lawrence Boadt's *Ezekiel's Oracles Against Egypt: A Literary and Philological Study of 29 – 32*, he says, "**Ezekiel's biting sarcasm** and his caricature of foreign beliefs accents the point that foreign myths do not reflect the true relationship of God and man, but only that of man exulting himself, the ultimate self-delusion" (p. 171). At https://books.google.com/books?id=-NDkUyV3oBsC&pg=PA171&lpg=PA171&dq=sarcasm+in+Ezekiel&source=bl&ots=edHdafyXEB&sig=cvZWHJMkRWhFbku2lgVdH_fe4wI&hl=en&sa=X&ei=7DGUVLjaL8mngwToxIPIDQ&ved=0CEcQ6AEwCA#v=onepage&q=sarcasm%20in%20Ezekiel&f=false.
    b. In *A New Heart: A Commentary on the Book of Ezekiel* by Bruce Vawter and Leslie J. Hope, the writers say, "In Ezek. 16:30-34 **in a piece of fine sarcasm** Ezekiel portrays Israel literally as a nymphomaniac whose promiscuous lust has caused her to reverse the usual order involved in prostitution" (p. 94). At: https://books.google.com/books?id=zKksNPzxgYwC&pg=PA94&lpg=PA94&dq=sarcasm+in+Ezekiel&source=bl&ots=Q0ZMDEJSGf&sig=Yz6_QyVyL5PV6le2v2-UH2Z_DRo&hl=en&sa=X&ei=_TiUVJHoDYmpgwSRqoHwCQ&ved=0CCYQ6AEwADgK#v=onepage&q=sarcasm%20in%20Ezekiel&f=false.

11. The definition of satire at: https://www.google.com/?gws_rd=ssl#q=define+satire.
12. The definition of mock at: https://www.google.com/?gws_rd=ssl#q=define+mock.
13. The word *hathal* at: http://www.blbclassic.org/lang/lexicon/lexicon.cfm?Strongs=H2048&t=KJV.
14. *Hebrew Word Pictures: How Does the Hebrew Alphabet Reveal Prophetic Truths?* by Dr. Frank T. Seekins (pages 10-11). Copyright © 2012 Frank T. Seekins. All Rights Reserved.
15. The word *sachaq* at: http://www.blbclassic.org/lang/lexicon/lexicon.cfm?Strongs=H7832&t=KJV.
16. Seekins pages 10-11.
17. The root word *la ag* at: http://www.blbclassic.org/lang/lexicon/lexicon.cfm?Strongs=H3932&t=KJV.
18. The word *la' eg* at: http://www.blbclassic.org/lang/lexicon/lexicon.cfm?Strongs=H3934&t=KJV.
19. The word *pharmakeia* at: http://www.blbclassic.org/lang/lexicon/lexicon.cfm?Strongs=G5331&t=KJV.

CHAPTER SIX

DANIEL: BUILD GOD'S EVERLASTING KINGDOM

"The God of heaven will set up another kingdom that will continue on forever.

It will never be destroyed. And it will be the kind of kingdom that cannot be passed on

to another group of people. This kingdom will crush all the other kingdoms.

It will bring them to an end, but that kingdom itself will continue forever"

Dan. 2:44 ERV

NO OTHER KINGDOM BUT THE KINGDOM OF GOD

Nebuchadnezzar had a dream with a huge statue of a man. Nebuchadnezzar called for his priests to interpret the dream, but he wouldn't tell them what the dream was. To be sure they were really able to interpret the meaning, he asked them to first recount the dream back to him. God did a miracle through Daniel—showing him what Nebuchadnezzar had seen.

In this dream the Lord disclosed to Nebuchadnezzar what would take place *"during the time of the kings of the fourth kingdom"* (Dan. 2:44a ERV). Nearly every Bible commentator agrees that this statue in King Nebuchadnezzar's dream represents four empires. The head of gold is Babylon, the breast and arms of silver are the Medes and Persians that would follow, the belly and thighs of bronze represent the next nation, Greece, and the lower legs and feet of iron and clay symbolize the Roman Empire that would come last.[1]

Daniel summed all this up beautifully when he interpreted Nebuchadnezzar's dream. Daniel told the king what he saw in the Spirit: *"**A stone was cut without hands**, by supernatural means. It struck the image on its feet of iron and clay and broke them to pieces. Then the iron, the clay, the bronze, the silver, and the gold were **together crushed to pieces**, and they became like the chaff of the summer threshing floors. And **the wind carried them away so not a trace of them could be found, scattered to oblivion, that no place was found for them, no sign of them was to be found. And the stone that struck the image became a great mountain and filled the whole earth"** (Dan. 2:34-35 HNV/NLT/NET/MSG/BBE).

Daniel continues to explain the dream to the king, *"**And in the day of those kings,** the God of Heaven shall set up a kingdom which shall never be destroyed.* **Which will never fall under the domination of other people, no one will ever conqueror it.** *It shall crush in pieces and make an end of all these kingdoms, shatter them into nothingness, and* **it shall come through it all standing strong and endure forever.** *The great God has made known to you what shall occur after this. And* **the dream is fixed and certain, and the meaning of it is trustworthy"** (Dan. 2:44-45 HNV/NLT/MSG/NASB/BBE). The kingdom represented by the feet of iron and clay is Rome (Dan. 7:7-14). During this period in history (when Rome was in power) is when God's Rock, Christ Jesus, came (Rom. 9:33). At His death on the Cross and His resurrection from the dead, Jesus, as the Rock, destroyed all the kingdoms of this world and their power and gave the kingdom to His saints (Dan. 7:26-27). This was the fulfillment of Nebuchadnezzar's dream.

With the resurrection of Jesus and His victory on the Cross, all the kingdoms of this world became like chaff blown away by the wind of the Spirit of God. There is not a trace left of them as far as the Lord is concerned. Jesus is the stone that struck the image (statue representing the kingdoms of this world) and His Kingdom will expand until it becomes *"a very large mountain and fill[s] up the whole earth"* (Dan. 2:35b ERV). The eyes of the Lord are only on His Rock—the Rock that shall come through it all standing strong and endure forever (Daniel 2:45). This rock

> At His death on the cross and resurrection from the grave Jesus destroyed all the kingdoms of this world

is continually growing and no one, not even the antichrist, will conquer or control it.

Read the Word of God again. The Lord says that it will *"never be destroyed, or fall under the dominion of other people, no one will ever conquer it. It will come through it all standing strong and endure forever."* The kingdom that Jesus began will stand forever, no one, including the antichrist, has the power to conquer it. This Word from the Lord is trustworthy—you can be confident it is true.

As God's warriors of love, He has commissioned us to take His Word to the nations. We are God's love warriors because the sole reason we conduct spiritual warfare comes as a result of our love for God and His children. We fight for the world because God loves the world (John 3:16). He has given us His specific prophetic words to destroy the demonic high places in the land and to set His children free from the forces of wickedness holding them in captivity. Once they are free, our divine mission is to then teach and disciple them in the love and ways of the Lord.

The Purpose of the Army of God

What is the purpose God has for His army? A beautiful picture of the Army of the Lord is seen in the army of David. The soldiers who came to enlist in David's army are a reflection of the Army of God. We read, *"More men joined David almost every day until he had a tremendous [and] great army—**like the army of God**"* (1 Chron. 12:22 TLB/NLT). What was their purpose? *"They were all equipped for war [and were] anxious to see David become king instead of Saul, just as the Lord said would happen"* (1 Chron. 12:23b TLB/GW). Later we read, *"All these men came in battle array to Hebron **with the single purpose, with a perfect heart, for the one reason to make David the king of Israel"*** (1 Chron. 12:38a TLB/ERV/NASB). David was already the king. He had been anointed to be king by the prophet Samuel years earlier before his family. But it was now time to make David king over all of Israel.

A study of 1 Chronicles 12 shows us that the characteristics of the army of David are awesome. It's vital for our survival to emulate them.[2] Like David's army, we also need to know our mission in the Army of God.

> *The single purpose of God's warriors of love is to make Jesus, God's anointed One, King over all*

All effective fighting forces have one goal, one mission. In the United States, our army produces soldiers to fight on land, our navy has sailors to protect our oceans, and our air force trains airmen to patrol the skies. They know their mission is to protect and defend the United States of America. What then is the goal, the clear mission for the warriors of God?

David's army knew their mission: *"They came to Hebron with a perfect heart, with one mind, both united and fully determined, **with the single purpose** to make David King of all Israel"* (1 Chron. 12:38 NGB/NIV/NASB/NLT/MSG). This is our mission. Our single purpose is to make Jesus Lord of all the earth. David had already been anointed to be king by the prophet Samuel years earlier, but now was the time for him to be acknowledged and made King of all Israel.[3] It is the same with Jesus, the Son of David. He is already anointed as King; it is now time for the whole world to acknowledge and accept Him as the King of kings and Lord of lords. What a glorious mission for us to fulfill as the warriors in God's Army!

The Big and Little Picture of God's Plan for the World

God has many plans and purposes for His children. We have just covered the big picture the Lord has for His earth—for every nation to come to the knowledge of His Son Jesus, that He is the Lord of lords and the King of kings. But first, every demonic stronghold over every nation must be attacked, killed, and buried under our feet.

Perhaps you find this idea too extreme, a little too absurd and unrealistic. If you believe my *big picture* claim to attack, kill, and bury demons is too absurd, let me ask you this question: "What is the *little picture* of God's plan for us individually?"

As I was driving into town one morning, the Lord gave me His answer for His plan for each one of us. He spoke two words into my spirit, "water baptism," and the revelation unfolded. What is God's purpose for each of us individually? The apostle Paul clearly tells us:

1. We all have an *"old man"* (Rom. 6:6, 7:5, Eph. 4:22, Col 3:9), also called the *"old creature"* (2 Cor. 5:17, Rom. 8:21, Gal. 5:15) that represents the *"flesh"* or our *"old sinful nature"* (2 Cor. 5:17; 10:3, Rom. 8:21, Gal. 5:15-19). The flesh is at war with our mind and spirit (Rom. 7:23-25). We must attack and resist the work of the flesh.

2. So what must we do with this old sinful nature? To have God's victory in our life, the Word of the Lord says that we kill it, crucify it. (Rom. 8:13, Gal. 2:20; & 5:24, Eph. 2:15). Paul tells us, *"So kill your earthly impulses... avoid them at all costs"* (Col. 3:5-6 Voice). We are to separate, cut off the deeds of darkness of the old nature; let them die.
3. And what do we do with a dead body? Why we bury it. We bury it in water baptism. (Matt. 28:18-20, Rom. 6:4; Col. 2:9-12).

To explain what I mean, let's look at what happens when we are baptized in water.

What happens at water baptism?

Something very important happens in the Spirit when we are baptized in water. This revelation is in the middle between the two extreme teachings on water baptism. On one end we have people teaching that water baptism is only an "act of faith and obedience" as we follow Jesus' example and His command to be baptized. Yes, it is an act of faith and obedience, but something much more significant happens to us than just getting wet as a symbol. This teaching does not go far enough.

On the other extreme is the teaching that our act of obedience in getting baptized will save us. It is taught that if we don't get baptized, we won't be saved. It is just like the days of Peter and Paul when religious men from Judah demanded that the Gentiles, the non-Jewish people who were coming to the Lord, must also be circumcised to be saved (Acts 15:1). Paul addresses this problem numerous times in his writings.

In his letter to the churches in Galatia he answers that there is no law we can obey that will make us right with God. If there was such a law that we could obey to make us righteous, *"then there was no need for Christ to die; then Christ died in vain"* (Gal. 2:21 NLT/NKJV). Jesus did not die in vain; we need His grace and mercy found in His shed blood! This second teaching focuses on "works," that there is something we can/must do that earns us our salvation. But we can't work to gain God's salvation. There is nothing we could ever do to earn or deserve it—it is a free gift from God (Eph. 2:8-9). This teaching on water baptism goes too far.

This second teaching goes too far and the first teaching doesn't go far enough. The truth is somewhere in the middle. Something beautiful happens when we are baptized. Paul says we must be circumcised, but he explains it's a spiritual circumcision.

Paul declares that we are all *"complete in Christ, Who is the Head of all principality and power:* **in Whom you are circumcised with the circumcision made without hands in putting off the body** *of the sins of the flesh; you were set free from your sinful nature by the circumcision of Christ"* (Col. 2:10-11 KJV/TLB/Phi/Nor). How then are we circumcised?

> Water baptism is a spiritual circumcision, God's operation "made without hands"

What is this *"circumcision of Christ"*? When does it happen? Paul explains, *"****Buried with Him in baptism;*** *you have been united with His burial, wherein also you* *are risen with Him* **through faith in the operation of God;** *Who has raised Him from the dead"* (Col. 2:12 KJV/Knox). At water baptism the *"operation of God"* is performed and our old sinful nature is cut off; we are circumcised spiritually. A funeral takes place as our old man is buried by *"the tremendous power of God"* (Col. 2:12 Phillips). We don't need a physical circumcision, we need a spiritual one, and it takes place on God's operating table at our water baptism.[4]

What happens at our water baptism gives us the victory. Paul explains to the believers at Rome, *"We have died to sin once and for all, as a dead man passes away from this life ... have you forgotten that* **all of us who were baptized into Jesus, the Anointed One, were baptized into His death? Sharing in His death by our baptism** *means that we were co-buried and entombed with Him, so that when the Father's glory raised Christ from the dead, we were also raised with Him.* **We have been co-resurrected with Him so that we could be empowered to express an entirely new life.** *Could it be any clearer that our old man is crucified with Him and is now and forever deprived of its power? For we were co-crucified with Him to* **dismantle the stronghold of sin within us**, *so that we would not continue to live one moment longer submitted to sin's power"* (Rom. 6:2-6 tPt/KJV). This is so good it's hard to stop! Read for yourself the rest of this chapter concerning the triumph of God's grace over sin.

Before we go on, I need to make a comment concerning infant baptism. It is a beautiful act of love as parents dedicate their children to the Lord. But I must ask anyone who has been baptized this way, "As a baby were you able to exercise your faith that God was cutting off your old nature when the priest (or minister) sprinkled you? Were you able to participate in this as an act of your will and obedience?" I encourage you to ask the Lord if you need to be water baptized again, this time with your faith actively, consciously engaged in what God is doing as you obey Him.

Now I can explain what I am teaching in this book of God's Lock and Load prophecies. This book gives the big picture on a national level that is a reflection of the little picture of what God does for all of us when we're born again. The big picture is just an expansion of the little picture. What God intends on the individual level, He also intends corporately on the national and international level. We must know what the Lord does for each of us personally, and then apply His victory strategy to the nations.

The Lock and Load Prophecies destroy national strongholds, so every nation can experience the new birth in Jesus

Once we have the victory in our own life, we can attack, kill, and bury the national strongholds over every country. When these strongholds are broken, the people of that country are then able to repent and come to the Father. As they repent, they attack, kill, and bury their own sinful natures and are raised in the newness of life as a new creation in Jesus. This is God's heart of war. He is the Divine "She-bear" (2 Sam. 17:8 Knox). The Lord has been robbed of His cubs, and He's come to rescue and set His baby cubs free!

OUR BAPTISM IS OUR ENLISTMENT INTO THE ARMY OF GOD

Every branch of the military has a "rite of passage," which is their basic training. Each member must successfully pass through it before they can enter into full service in their specific military force. Jesus set the example for us.

After Jesus was baptized by John in the Jordan River what happened to Him immediately afterwards? He went into the wilderness and began to take on the enemy in His boot camp in the desert, right after His baptism, *"the Holy Spirit led Jesus into the lonely wilderness* **in order to reveal His strength against the devil by going through the ordeal of testing."** (Matt. 4:1-2 tPt footnote; Luke 4:1). Water Baptism is the first step of our rite of passage into the wilderness; it is basic training for the Army of God.

Hear what Paul says in the context of water baptism in his letter to the church in the city of Colossae: *"Thank You Father...***You have rescued us from dark powers** *and brought us safely into the kingdom of Your Son"* (Col. 1:12-13 Voice). *"God was pleased that all His fullness should forever dwell in His Son,* **Who bled peace into the world by His death on the Cross** *as God's means of reconciling the whole creation to Himself"*(Col. 1:19-20 Voice). Paul continues to explain, *"****This battle I am facing is huge.*** *And, I want you to know, I do it for you"* (Col. 2:1 Voice). He adds a warning, *"***Make sure no predator makes you his prey by philosophy***, intellectualism, and some high-sounding nonsense about the nature of the universe, instead of following what Christ has taught. For they operate with humanistic and clouded judgments based on the mindset of this world system, and not the anointed truths of the Anointed One"* (Col. 2:8 Voice/Phi/Noli/CTB/tPt). Paul is not finished.

He goes on to declare that Jesus *"***has disarmed those who once ruled over us***—those who had overpowered us.* **Like captives of war,** *He put them on display to the world to show*

His victory over them by means of the cross. He was not their prisoner; they were His!" (Col. 2:15 Voice/tPt). Do you hear what Paul is saying? It is a huge battle we are facing to set the prisoners of war free, but the Lord Jesus has given us the power and the victory. Jesus conquers and captivates those who once held us captive.

GOD'S HOLY GHOST "EARTH PROJECT"

What are the plans, the purposes of God? What is His "earth project"? Psalm 92 shows God's plans so well that you need to stop and read the whole Psalm. Here are a few highlights:

> *"It is good to say, 'Thank You" to the Lord, to sing praises to* **the God, Who is above all gods.**
>
> *Every morning tell Him, 'Thank You for Your kindness,' and every evening rejoice in His faithfulness.*
>
> *How great are Your works, O Lord!* **Your plans are very deep [and] intricate!**
>
> *The Lord continues forever, exalted in the heavens,* **while His enemies shall disappear** *[and] be scattered.*
>
> **But You have made me as strong as a charging wild bull; I have been anointed with fresh oil; You've empowered my life for triumph.** *How refreshed I am by Your power!*
>
> **My eyes have seen the defeat and downfall of my adversaries; with my own ears have heard of the defeat [and] doom of my wicked and evil assailants. and I've heard the cries of their surrender!**

> *But the godly shall flourish like the palm trees,* and grow tall as the cedars of Lebanon. ***They are transplanted into the Lord's own garden, and thriving under His personal care.***
>
> This honors the Lord, and exhibits His faithful care.
>
> ***He is my shelter.*** There is nothing but goodness in Him!"

A summary of this Psalm is that in thankful worship we receive revelations of His thoughts, plans, and purposes. They are deep and intricate. The Hebrew word for deep is *amaq* and a possible letter by letter definition is "to see or experience chaos put behind us."[5] God's deep thoughts and plans are to destroy the plans of the enemy and put his chaos behind us. God makes us like trees planted in His garden, protected under His personal care. The Lord anoints us and makes us His *wild ox*. As God's wild ox we are *"refreshed by His power"* to tread upon our spiritual enemies and trample down their chaos under our feet forever (Num. 23:22; 24:8, Mic. 4:13).

> *God's plan is to destroy the devil's plans—to bury the evil one under our feet forever as we are refreshed by God's power*

ENDNOTES

1. *Deluxe Then and Now Bible Maps.* (Hong Kong: Rose Publishing, 2015), p. 21.
2. As we study 1 Chronicles 12 we see some interesting characteristics of the soldiers in David's army. The characteristics of these warriors reflect the soldiers in God's army:
   a. *"They could sling stones and shoot arrows with either their right hands or their left hands"* (1 Chron. 12:2 NGB). This reminds us of Paul's exhortation, *"We have faithfully preached the word of truth, in the power of God working in us; by all the godly man's arsenal—**the weapons of righteousness, a sword in one hand and a shield in the other for both the right hand and the left**"*(2 Cor. 6:7 NLT/TLB/NASB/tPt).
   b. *"They were warriors, trained soldiers, able to fight with shield and spear.* ***They looked like lions and they were fast as deer on the mountains"*** (1 Chron. 12:8 NGB/NLT). This is a reference that they looked like the Lion of the tribe of Judah (Praise) and the deer remind us of the prophet Habakkuk, where he says *"the Lord GOD is my strength. He makes my feet like those of a deer. He makes me tread upon the high places"* (Hab. 3:19b NGB/KJV/NRSV).
   c. *"The least able one could take on, was a match for 100 men, and the greatest was able to resist, was able to take on a 1,000 men"* (1 Chron. 12:14 NGB/KJV/NASB/NLT/NIV). Here we're reminded of the promise of God that *"there will be peace in your land,* ***no one will scare or terrify you.*** *You will chase your enemies, and you will defeat them. Five of you will chase a 100 of them, and a 100 of you will chase 10,000 of them! All your enemies will fall beneath the blows of your weapons"* (Lev. 26:6-8 NGB/NET/NLT).
   d. ***"They understand the times*** *and know what was best for Israel to do"* (1 Chron. 12:32 NGB/BBE). How we need this Divine wisdom in our warfare today!
   e. *"They are experienced soldiers, equipped for battle* ***with every kind of weapon.*** *Their loyalty was unquestioned, [with]* ***an undivided heart and singleness of purpose.*** *They were stout-hearted men who could keep ranks.* ***They were ready to fight with all kinds of weapons of war"*** (1 Chron. 12:33-37 NGB/NASB/NRSV/MSG). This is the reason for *God's Heart of War Series.* We have more weapons at our disposal than just the sword of the Spirit; we have God's War Cries, War Flags, War Horn, War Songs, War Bow and Arrows ... just to name a few that are contained in the Arsenal of God. We must know about all of these weapons, what they do and how and when to use them. Our survival depends upon us knowing them all and how to use them.
3. David's Three-fold Anointing as King David was anointed three times before he was accepted as the king of Israel.
   a. The first time was by the prophet Samuel in front of David's family (1 Sam. 16:13).

b. The second time made him king over the tribe of Judah, the people of praise (2 Sam. 2:4).
   c. The third and last time was over the whole nation of Israel at Hebron (2 Sam. 5:1-6). After the first anointing, David did not automatically take the throne in Jerusalem. There was a progression in his life before he finally became King of Israel. David started with his family then he was acknowledged by Judah, the tribe of praise, and finally by the whole nation of Israel. There is a similar progression with Jesus as the Messiah. Jesus starts with His family, then moves on to His praisers, and finally to Israel and all the nations of the world.
4. I need to give credit to Bob and Rose Wiener for this revelation on water baptism. They have been teaching this victorious revelation since the early 1970s. The Body of Christ needs to hear this beautiful picture of what happens as we obey in faith the command of Jesus to be baptized. At water baptism our old sinful nature is cut away and killed. We leave it behind, buried in our watery grave, as we rise up to walk in our new life as God's new creation in Christ Jesus. Such a practical act of faith has a powerful impact in our life.
5. Seekins, pages 10-11.

CHAPTER SEVEN

OUR FOUR-PRONGED ATTACK

*"For **this is the purpose** why Jesus was manifested, that He might destroy and **put an end to the works of the devil**"*

1 John 3:8b KJV/BBE

OUR FOUR-PRONGED STRATEGY

God has a divine, four-pronged strategy for us as we advance and attack our spiritual adversaries. All the weapons we use involve the Word of God in our warfare-worship (Psa. 18:34 tPt).

1. **Sing the Taunting War Songs of Isaiah**

    Our first assault is to use the War Songs of God as we shout, shoot, and sing God's Word of victory He has given us in Jesus. We sing these War Songs as we attack our adversaries. We declare their doom, defeat, and destruction as we taunt and pierce them with the Word of God.

2. **Wail the Sarcastic Lamentations of Jeremiah**

    Second, we follow up with God's sarcastic lamentations of the separation from and death of our demonic oppressors to completely cut off their influence over us. We wail them sarcastically. As we *sarkazein* the Lamentations of God, we are cutting off the flesh of the old nature from our lives and the lives of others. This is possible because at the cross our flesh is crucified with Christ and dies. At our water baptism the old nature is buried, and we are free to bring deeds of light.

3. **Chant the Mocking Dirges of Ezekiel**

    Third, we chant dirges of God as we bury the demons at their funeral—when they are placed under our feet forever. We tread upon their heads as we mockingly chant the Dirges of the Lord in our praise and worship. By the Spirit of God, we dance on their graves.

4. **Proclaim God's Words of Victory Fulfilling Daniel's Vision**

    Last of all, we have the honor to profess God's Words of victory and hope over us and those who have been bound by the evil one. God's purpose for us is to fulfill the vision the Lord gave to Daniel. We are used by God as He takes the Rock, Christ Jesus, and shatters all the earthly kingdoms. As we sing, the Lord causes the kingdom of Jesus to grow until it becomes a mountain that covers the whole earth (Dan. 2:34-45).

> *As we sing and dance in our warfare-worship, we tread on the head of our adversary*

The Ever Expanding Kingdom of God

First, before we can rise up with the weapons the Lord has put at our disposal, we must learn what they do and how to use them. Only after we are trained and battle-ready can we attack. But when (and only when) the Lord gives us the command, do we attack the strongholds holding His people captive. Second, we support Israel in the spiritual realm against forces of darkness who still dwell in that region and wish to see her destroyed. And third, we release all the nations of the world. Our mission is to confront and destroy these spiritual, national strongholds which are set against the Church and Israel.

This is the divine plan of the Lord as He spoke it through Jesus, *"And you shall be My witnesses both in Jerusalem, and all Judea, and in Samaria, and unto the uttermost part of the earth"* (Acts 1:8 NASB). We can only do this by the Word of God, under the anointing of His Holy Spirit, through the power of the name of, and by the blood of the Lamb.

The Outline of Volume Two

We have come to the end of the introduction of *The Lock and Load Prophecies of God,* and a solid foundation has been laid. This was vital to your understanding and ability to execute God's strategy for war against the enemy. In Volume Two (the next book of the Lock and Load Prophecies of God), each chapter will include four sections.

- **Section One will cover the problem.** We will identify the demonic stronghold and the signs and symptoms that manifest its deadly infections.

- **Section Two will cover God's solutions.** We will study the specific prophetic words God has spoken against that stronghold and how we can defeat it. These prophetic word weapons are His War Songs, Lamentations, and Dirges.

- **Section Three will cover God's vision of victory.** This is where we'll discover God's calling for that nation. Once its people are set free they can walk in their destiny—a future full of hope that He has for them.

- **Section Four will give examples of God's Word set to music that we may sing, wail, and chant.** As we sing the Word of God, the Rock *"cut out without hands ... [will] become a great mountain and [fill] the whole earth"* (Dan. 2:34-35 NKJV). We will apply these truths for victory for the Church, Israel, and all the nations of the world.

Some examples of the spiritual strongholds we are called to destroy are the demonic forces of perpetual hatred and unforgiveness, sex trafficking, the spirit of poverty and failure, spiritual and sexual perversion, and unholy pride to name a few. As God's children, we are called to attack, kill, and bury them. Our mission in life is to be a part of the Father God's army to fulfill His plan to put every enemy under the feet of Jesus.

Like Deborah: Celebrate and Sing God's Victory Songs!

I would like to give a word of encouragement to the women reading this book. If you reading a book like this, it is probably because you are an intercessor, and you may be asking why are these War Songs, lamentations, and dirges so important? They are important because they are victory songs expressing the triumph of our King. They are songs, like the Song of Deborah, reminding us of God's power. They are for all of us, especially women, to sing.

In the book of Judges, the Israelites go to battle against the Canaanites and win. Victory comes as the result of the faith-filled actions of two women: Deborah and Jael. Women are vital warriors in the Army of God.

Listen to Deborah as she sings her victory song: *"When all hell breaks loose Israel's leaders take charge.* **The people gladly follow and answered the call to war**—*Praise the Lord! ...* **Warriors were scarce in Israel, until you arose, Deborah, until you arose as a motherly protector in Israel** *... My heart went out to Israel's leaders, to the willing volunteers who answered the call to war. Praise the Lord! ...* **The Lord's people came down to me as warriors ... The most rewarded of women should be Jael** *... She hammered Sisera, she shattered his skull, she smashed his head, she drove the tent peg through his temple"* (Jud. 5:1-2, 7, 9, 13, 25-26 Fox footnote/NET/NLT). Women of God you play a very important part in God's Army. The Lord calls you a *mother of Israel*.

The Mothers of Israel

As a daughter of God, God calls you a mother of Israel like Deborah. While in the assembly of warfare-worship, you lead the way singing victory songs to the King. Maybe up until this time *warriors were scarce* in your church, but as you begin to sing God's Prophetic Words, faith arises in the hearts of the hearers, and *the Lord's people [come] down to [you] as warriors*. Like Deborah, your victory songs produce victorious soldiers. The most honored of those who respond and come down will be women warriors like Jael.

You are a mother of Israel like Jael; you know your position of power in God. When the enemy shows up at your doorstep, you do not scream and hide. No! You smile and say, "Come inside, I have something special for you." You are safe and secure for the blood of the Lamb covers your home. The tent pegs supporting your home are like the nails from Jesus' cross.

You ask Jesus if you may borrow one of His nails for a moment. The enemy is attacking your homeland and has now shown up at your front door. You want to give him a *royal welcome* in Jesus' name. You take that nail and drive it through the devil's head, until he's dead stretched out like a bearskin rug on your living room floor.[1] You thank Jesus as you return His nail, and from that day forward you walk on the devil's head as you go about your daily business. You and your family are safe in Jesus.

This is why women sing the War Songs, lamentations, and dirges of God!

IT'S TIME TO GET OUR ACT TOGETHER

Before any of this can happen, we as the Body of Christ must get our act together. The Lord calls His Church, the Body of Christ, to be three things: a home, a temple, and an army. As you may have guessed, this book is about the army. But the members of His army must love each other like a family as the battle we wage for the world is expressed in our warfare-worship of love.

> God's *army must love each other like a family as we fight for the salvation of the world*

But just like the military in the natural realm, you don't recruit and train people who are sick or weak. Soldiers need to be healthy and strong. This doesn't mean we have to wait until we are perfect before we can join: the only One who is perfect in the Army of God is Jesus, our Commander and Chief. We just need to be ready and willing to obey the orders of our Lord. By the grace of God, we are able to sing, **"Lord we are able.** *Our spirits are Thine. Remold them, make us, like Thee, divine ... To the death we follow Thee."*[2] What a glorious hymn to sing today!

The natural military can't use anyone who is unfit. If a person is weak or sick—mentally, physically, or emotionally—the military will not allow them to enlist. If they become this way after they are enrolled and they are unable to become healthy and whole with reasonable support, the military will discharge them. They cannot fight. They would become a liability to both themselves and the mission. However, in the Army of God, if anyone is weak or sick, we must let them bask in the presence of the Lord and minister to them until they are healed in every area they are affected. They will never be discharged as unfit, but neither will they be put on the front lines: they will be brought to healing. If you feel too wounded or broken to fight, go and seek out other mature men and women of God to help get you back on your feet. Let the healing power of God set you free, make you whole again. Once you are well, come on in and let your training of love begin!

GOD'S SPIRITUAL BOOT CAMP

If we are weak, we need to "work out" in the Spirit. As Jude tells us, *"Build yourself up in your most holy faith, praying in the power of the Holy Ghost"* (Jude 1:20 KJV/NEB), grow strong enough to be an asset and not a liability. Praying in the Holy Ghost is not an option; it is vital for our survival.

If anyone has not been baptized in the Holy Ghost, ask the Lord for this precious gift (Acts 11:44-48). In the days ahead we are going to need to *"be endued and **armed** with the power from on high"* that Jesus promises us as we're clothed with the Holy Ghost (Luke 24:49 KJV/NEB). We need all the power from above that we can get!

> *In the days ahead, we need all the power from on high we can get!*

When I joined the Marine Corps back in 1970 I had asthma. If I tried to join today they wouldn't let me in, but back then, during the Vietnam War, they'd take anyone who had a pulse! I couldn't run three hundred yards without running out of breath and experiencing an asthma attack, much less run three miles! But in boot camp the Marines trained us slowly and had us run a little farther each week. As a result, I grew stronger each day. Before I knew it, I could easily run those three miles.

There were a few soldiers in our platoon who needed more time to increase their strength and stamina, so their basic training was put on hold. They were reassigned to the fitness platoon. All day long they'd just work out for as long as it took until they were strong enough to handle the stressful rigors of basic training.

The Marines would take whatever time they needed to get those soldiers strong enough to handle basic training. It is the same in God's Army. We don't have to be supermen and women, we just need to be healthy enough to handle and survive the challenging experiences of God's boot camp, His wilderness experience for us. How long do we need to be trained? That depends on us and our faith in the Lord. For Jesus it only took 40 days (Matt. 4:1-2), for Paul it took 3 years (Gal. 1:15-18), and for the children of Israel it took 40 years (Deut. 2:7). The whole purpose of our wilderness boot camp is to learn to trust the Lord in all things.

Once we're secure in Jesus, we're ready for God's next step. The Marines made boot camp very, very tough. Why? Because by just going through that training, we were made strong enough to handle whatever our opponents might throw at us later on in a real fire fight.

Once we are strong, healthy, and graduate from boot camp, then it's time to start our specialized training. In the Marine Corps, after boot camp at Paris Island, we were sent to another Marine base. There we'd focus on the specific battle skills needed to be prepared for what we'd been assigned to fulfill.

The Wilderness is God's Boot Camp

The wilderness is God's boot camp. As mentioned earlier, it took the Israelites forty years to graduate (Deut. 2:7), but Jesus only took forty days (Matt. 4:1-11 and Luke 4:1-14). What is the purpose of the wilderness? God told Israel, *"Remember how the LORD your God lead you through the wilderness for forty years, humbling you, **testing you to prove your character**, to know what you were made of, what was in your hearts and **to find out whether you would keep His orders or not"*** (Deut. 8:2 NIV/NLT/MSG/BBE). The wilderness proves our character and trains us to keep His orders. Once that is accomplished, we're prepared to do battle and take our Promised Land.

The Lord spoke through Amos and said, *"I brought you up from the land of Egypt; I led you through the wilderness for forty years **so you could take the Amorites' land as your own"*** (Amos 2:10 NET). This is the reason for God's wilderness boot camp. The training prepares us so we are able to take our Promised Land. According to Jesus, our Promised Land is the whole world. He commissions us to *"make disciples of all the nations"* (Matt. 28:19-20 ASV).

If we survive God's bootcamp, we can survive anything

The Spiritual Forces Against Israel

The Lord has called us to support and stand in the gap for the nation of Israel. Just as it was 2,000 years ago, many

OUR FOUR-PRONGED ATTACK | 113

nations today want to see Israel destroyed and driven into the sea.

This map shows ancient Israel during the time of the divided kingdom of Israel. We see that Israel is literally surrounded by six nations. Starting in the northwest and going clock-wise around to the southwest we see: the Phoenicians (or Lebanon), Aram (Syria), Ammon, and Moab (both are now Jordan), Edom (now in Saudi Arabia), and the Philistines (or Palestine).³ The demonic forces ruling those six nations want to see Israel destroyed. These spirits are still operating today and trying to control the people in those same areas.

There are other nations in the Ancient Middle East that were enemies of Israel. The next map is an expanded area of the Ancient Near East (ANE) showing more of Israel's opponents. In this map we see fourteen more nations hostile to Israel. They are Amalek, Egypt, Midian, Cush (Ethiopia), Greece, Tubal, Meshech, Arabia, Kedar, Babylon (Chaldea), Assyria, Elam, the Medes (Media), and Persians.[4] The principalities and powers ruling these nations also want to annihilate the chosen people of God. The names of the nations may have changed, but the same demonic strongholds are still there and still trying to destroy Israel.

That's over 20 countries who, at one time or the other, have been adversaries against the land of Israel. It hasn't changed much. In this book we only have space to address eight of them, and God's Word of victory concerning the future of these nations along with Israel.

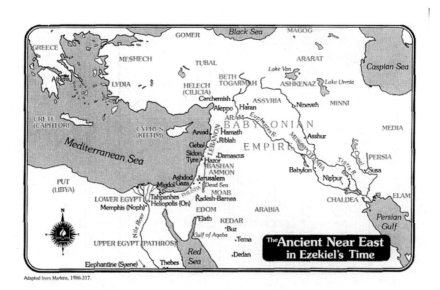

Adapted from Martens, 1986:317.

Comparison of the ancient Middle East nations with today's Middle East nations

Old Testament Names	Modern Day Name
Phoenicia	Lebanon
Moab	Jordan
Ammon	Jordan
Aram	Syria
Babylon and Assyria	Iraq, Iran, Saudia Arabia
Amalek and Midian	Sinai Peninsula of Egypt
Cush	Ethiopia
Elam Medes and Persians	Iran, Afghanistan, Pakistan
Philistia	The Gaza Strip
Edom	Saudia Arabia

Nearly all the modern countries listed on the right column still hate the Jewish people. They would throw a party and rejoice if Israel was cast into the sea. Those same demonic spirits are still working in these regions today. They must be attacked, killed, and buried before we will ever have peace in the Middle East.

These unclean spirits are not limited to the Middle East. They are found all over the world, and as enemies of God they must be defeated. This is not a job that a natural army can accomplish. It will only be done by God's spiritual army using the spiritual weapons out of God's arsenal. Listen to the prophets Jeremiah, *"The **Lord has opened His arsenal** and brought out **weapons to explode His wrath upon His enemies**"* (Jer. 50:25 KJV/Sprl/TLB); and Isaiah, *"It is the Lord with **the weapons of His wrath** coming against you, O Babylon to destroy your whole land"* (Isa. 13:5 KJV/NEB/TLB). You have to love the phrase *"weapons to explode His wrath."* It is God's wrath exploding on the devil and his demons, that we have the honor to release.

There is one last vital aspect to God's call on His army. Just as these strongholds are set against Israel, they also hate and oppress His Church. These same demonic forces harass and attack the followers of Jesus. We are called to defend not only Israel, but every nation including our own. We're called to defeat these unclean spirits, and God has given us the power to do it.

God's Professional Killers in the Human Body

After I retired from the military, I was able to go back to college on the GI Bill. It was available for anyone who served during the War on Terror. I was always asking the Lord to reveal His truth in the classes I was taking, and it was awesome.

In one class on anatomy and physiology, the textbook had a section on the immune system that God has created and placed in our body to protect us from invading pathogens such as bacteria, viruses, and cancer. As I read this chapter I felt like I was back in the Marines reading a manual on military strategy and tactics for war. Let me give you some exact quotes from the textbook and explain what I mean.

Our immune system was created by God to maintain hemostasis (balance) in our body. Our textbook said the immune system *"recognizes, attacks, and destroys foreign agents in the body. Obviously, this is important because **the body is constantly under attack** from foreign agents (e.g. bacteria, viruses, and fungi) that promote infection."* Our immune system is composed of many different specialized cells that fight for our health.

Here are some of the cells in our immune system God has designed to protect our body:

1. Macrophages which engulf and destroy bacteria. They *"recruit other immune system players* **to the battle site** *to assist in protecting the body."* There is a spiritual war going on around us, and a biological battle being fought inside of us!

2. Neutrophils which are *"called* **professional killers** *that are 'on call' in the blood."* Notice that these professional killers exist **in the blood** until they're called upon to fight.

3. A third group of cells are called *"natural killer cells."* When they are *"called to fight an infection, these* **cells exit the blood and move to the battleground** *to take part in the fight."* God has naturally equipped our body to protect itself against foreign invaders.

The reason many of these cells are called natural, professional killers is because *"they* **make their living attacking"** invading pathogens.

The last group called, "natural killer cells" are divided into three types:

A. *"Killer T cells* **are a potent weapon** *against viruses because they can* **recognize and kill** *virus-infected cells."*

B. *"Helper T cells ... serve as the quarterback of the immune system* **by directing the action of the other immune cells."**

C. "Regulatory T cells play a vital role in **preventing the immune system from attacking normal body cells.**"[5] In other words this third group prevents the body from attacking itself.

Putting all of this together gives us a beautiful picture of God's strategic plans for protecting the Body of Christ.

GOD'S KILLER I (INTERCESSOR) CELLS IN THE BODY OF CHRIST

How does this relate to us in the Kingdom of God? It tells us that the Lord has created specific cells in our body whose sole purpose is to recognize, attack, and destroy invading pathogens in our natural body. If God has done this for our natural body, then how much more has He created *professional killers* in the Body of Christ! God has called everyone who is a prayer warrior to be His *Killer I cells*. The letter "I" stands for intercessor, God's Killer Intercessors.

You are His natural-born, professional killers that recognize, attack, and drive out every foreign invader in His spiritual body. The whole purpose of our existence is to recognize, attack, and kill any unholy pathogen that attempts to make the Lord's body—His Church—weak and sick. As prayer warriors, our job is to identify and attack the enemy who's invading the Body of Christ. They want to make it so sick that its members attack one another.

Go back and read those textbook quotations again, especially the bold print phrases, and see how this directly applies to us in our spiritual warfare. This all makes sense when we realize that the word immune comes "from the Latin term *immunitas* (meaning 'freedom from')."[6] Everyone who has been called by God to be an intercessor is a member of His Freedom Fighters, one of His natural, professional killers to recognize, attack, and destroy the works of the devil and set the Body of Christ free from his poisonous lies!

> *Intercessors and prayer warriors are God's professional killers who protect the body of Christ—His Holy Ghost freedom fighters!*

ENDNOTES

1. In the footnote to this story of Jael, in Robert Alter's translation of Judges, he says it is ironic as Jael plays the role of a mother to an enemy general who is killing her people. He explains, "Jael's playing a maternal role towards the man she is about to kill: first she covers him with a blanket, then gives him milk to drink and readjusts the blanket." As he sleeps, she goes and gets her hammer and nail! You have to love this! Jael as a mother of Israel deceives the deceiver; she tricks the trickster and has the last laugh as she nails his head to the floor. The Lord enjoys turning the tables on the evil one. The great deceiver and trickster is tricked and reaps the deception he has sown. Robert Alter, *Ancient Israel-The Former Prophets: Joshua, Judges, Samuel, and Kings*, (New York: W. W. Norton & Company, 2013) p.129.
2. Lyrics to the Hymn *Are ye Able* by Earl Marlatt, music by Harry S. Mason at: http://www.hymnsite.com/lyrics/umh530.sht.
3. Map of Israel during the Old Testament at: https://www.pinterest.com/pin/282249101622163293/.
4. Map of the Ancient Near East at: http://www.ldslastdays.com/default.aspx?page=pscbofa.htm.
5. Scott K. Powers and Edward T. Howley, "*Exercise Physiology: Theory and Application to Fitness and Performance,*" 8th Ed. (New York: McGraw Hill, 2012) pp. 127-133.
6. Ibid. page 127.

CONCLUSION

DESTROY STRONGHOLDS AND DISCIPLE NATIONS

*"The seventy disciples came back triumphant
and with joy reported to Him,
'Lord even the demons obey us when we use Your name.'
Jesus said, 'I saw satan fall from heaven like a lightning bolt …'*
**Then Jesus Himself became elated.
The Holy Spirit was on Him,
and He began to pray with joy."**

Luke 10:17-18a & 21b NLT/MSG/Voice

LET'S CAUSE JESUS TO PRAY WITH JOY!

When the disciples returned to Jesus full of joy because the demons obeyed them *"then Jesus Himself became elated … and **began to pray with joy**"* (Luke 10:21 Voice).

This is one of my goals in life. To act and speak in such a way it causes Jesus to pray with joy!

Jesus is the *"High Priest of our confession"* (Heb. 3:1 NASB). As our High Priest, Jesus sits at the right hand of the Father interceding for us (Rom. 8:34). He stands in the gap as the Mediator between God and His people. As the High Priest of our confession, Jesus tells the Father God what His children are saying. Let what we say cause Jesus (as our High Priest) to pray with joy.

If we complain, then that is what Jesus as our High Priest repeats to the Father. One example is when the Israelites complained to Moses about having no meat to eat in the wilderness; all they had was manna (Num. 11:4-6). When Moses prayed to the Lord he said, *"They keep whining for meat, but where can I get meat for them?"* (Num. 11:13a CEV). So it is today, if we complain, the words of our confession, our complaint is the only thing Jesus can repeat to the Father.

At least Moses asked God where he could get the meat for the Israelites, and the Lord was able to give him an answer. But what happens if we confess the Word of God instead of complaining about our situation? Instead of whining and worrying about what is going on in the world, let us confess His promises thanking Him in advance for His victory!

What better words to confess to our Great High Priest than the Word of the Lord? When we see demonic activity in a region, just like the disciples, we come in the Name of Jesus and stand on the Word of God. We confess with faith what God says about our situation.

As we sing God's Word against that demonic stronghold, Jesus repeats our confession of faith to the Father and prays with joy! God the Father works with our words of faith.

He moves into action with a smile as He commands His angels, His *"powerful warriors who carry out His plans, waiting for His voice and do what He says"* (Psa. 103:20 NET/NLT/BBE/MSG). They obey His voice, and the Father rejoices as His voice of destruction shatters every ungodly chain of bondage.

Sing the Word of God—cause Jesus our High Priest to pray to the Father with joy

Jesus Commissions His Church

At the end of each Gospel story Jesus gives us a beautiful revelation of God's purpose for the Church. In Matthew He issues His **Great Commission:** *"Go and **make disciples of all the nations"*** (Matt. 28:19-20 ASV). In Mark He proclaims **God's Confirmation** of our actions, *"In My name you will cast out demons, they will speak in new tongues… they will lay hands on the sick and they shall recover. And they went forth, and preached everywhere, the Lord working with them, and **confirming the word with signs following"*** (Mark 16:17-20 KJV). In Luke, Jesus gives us the promise of **God's Companion** as we are *"endued, clothed or **armed with power from on high"*** (Luke 24:49 KJV/ASV/NEB). It is by the anointing of the Holy Spirit, Who works and fights through us, that we win the victory. And last of all in John, Jesus instructs us to go in **God's Compassion.** We are told to do all of this in the love of God. If we love Jesus and the Father, we'll love His children. When Jesus asks us *"Do you love Me?"* (John 21:15-17 KJV), and we answer "Yes." He responds and tells us to *"Feed My lambs … Feed My sheep"* (John 21:15-17 KJV). Everything we do must be done in the power of God's Word and in the anointing of His Spirit and love.

In summary we see that Matthew gives us the Commission, Mark gives us the Confirmation, Luke gives us the Companion, and John gives us the Compassion. We must live in all four areas if we want to see the Kingdom of God come and His will be done on earth as it's done in heaven.

We Must Destroy the Strongholds Before We Fully Disciple the Nations

We have been called to make disciples of all the nations, but there are barriers in the way. There are spiritual strongholds that need to be torn down. Just like the battle of Jericho, we do what we need to do to release the light and glory of God on a nation. After the walls fall down and every obstacle is removed, then we have the freedom to minister to those in that land.

I can't wait until you can read Volume Two of *The Lock and Load Prophecies of God!* In the next volume we'll discover God's Words of victory over demonic strongholds and His glorious destiny awaiting the people who are set free!

Here are a few examples of what is covered in Volume Two concerning God's victory over:

1. **Shame**: God heals those oppressed by shame and restores them as a child of God. They forget the past and are made His warrior.
2. **Sorcery**: God transforms demon worshippers into His worship leaders.

3. **Sexual Addictions**: God breaks their chains of sexual perversions and calls them to build His house.
4. **Poverty and Failure**: God takes the poor and lowly and commissions them to be part of His burial crew to dig the devil's grave.
5. **Terrorism**: God changes the land of violence into His headquarters for the Gospel.

After the strongholds fall before us as we sing the Word of God, the prisoners are set free to follow Jesus. He comes and takes up residence as Lord and King. As Micah prophesies, *"The Breaker [the Messiah] will go before them. They will break out of the city gates where they've been held captive and go free. The Lord Himself, their rightful King will show the way and lead them"* (Mic. 2:13 AMP/Voice/CW). Before our Breaker King the gates come crashing down!

> We break out of the city gates and
> go free as our King leads the way!

APPENDIX A

List of the Lock and Load Prophecies of God

Note: The prophecies are listed according to the prophet who spoke them against the demonic strongholds ruling over that nation. This list is incomplete, there are many more in the Word of God.

Prophets in the Old Testament

Reference	Nation/City/Individual
Elijah	
1. 2 Kings 9:1-37 (vs. 25 with 1 Kings 21:1-29)	King Ahab and Queen Jezebel
Isaiah	
2. 11:10-16	God's introductory warning to the nations
3. 13:1-14:23	Babylon and Lucifer

4.	14:24-27	Assyria
5.	14:28-32	Philistia
6.	15:1-16:14	Moab
7.	17:1-14	Damascus/Syria (Aram)
8.	18:1-7	Cush (Ethiopia)
9.	19:1-25	Egypt
10.	20:1-6	Egypt and Cush
11.	21:1-10	Babylon, the "Desert by the sea"
12.	21:11-12	Edom (Dumah/Seir)
13.	21:13-17	Arabia (Kedar)
14.	22:1-14	Jerusalem, the "Valley of Vision"
15.	22:15-25	Jesus became sin on the Cross
16.	23:1-8	Tyre
17.	24:1-25:8	Conclusion to chapters 13-23
18.	25:9-12	Moab
19.	26:1-21	Judah's song of rejoicing
20.	27:1	God slays Leviathan
21.	27:2-13	Song of the Vineyard
22.	28:1-29	Gift of Speaking in Tongues (God's Rest)
23.	29:1-30:5	Jerusalem and Israel
24.	30:6-26	Beasts of the Negev (the Amalekites), Egypt and Israel
25.	30:27-33	Assyria

26.	31:1-33:24	Israel
27.	34:1-17	Edom (representing all the nations)
28.	35:1-10	Zion rejoices
29.	37:21-38	Sennacherib King of Assyria
30.	40:1-45:25	Israel and her Warrior King of Salvation
31.	46:1-47:15	Fall of Babylon (Bel and Nebo)
32.	48:1-66:24	God's Suffering Savior and Israel's restoration

Jeremiah's Word to the Nations (46:1)

33.	9:25-26	God's roar
34.	25:13-38	God's introductory warning to the nations

Jeremiah continued

35.	46:2-28	Egypt
36.	47:1-7	Philistia
37.	48:1-47	Moab
38.	49:1-6	Ammon
39.	49:7-22	Edom
40.	49:23-27	Damascus (Syria)
41.	49:28-33	Arabia (Kedar and Hazor)
42.	49:34-39	Elam
43.	50:1-51:64	Babylon

Ezekiel

44.	18:1-19:14	Israel
45.	21:28	Ammon
46.	25:1-7	Ammon
47.	25:8-11	Moab
48.	25:12-14	Edom
49.	25:15-17	Philistia
50.	26:1-28:19	Tyre and lucifer
51.	28:20-26	Sidon
52.	29:1-32:32	Egypt/Ethiopia (Cush)
53.	35:1-15	Edom
54.	37:1-28	The Valley of Dry Bones
55.	38:1-39:29	Gog and Magog

Daniel

56.	2:1-49	Destiny of the Nations (Babylon, Greece, Medes/Persians & Rome)
57.	8:1-27	Greece and Medes-Persians
58.	11:2-4	Greece and Medes-Persians
59.	11:5-35	Egypt and Syria
60.	11:36-45	Antichrist

Hosea

61.	1:1-14:9	God wooing Israel, His bride, back to Himself

Joel

- 62. 1:1-2:32   Judah
- 63. 3:1-15   Tyre/Sidon, Philistia, Greece and Sabeans (Sheba),
- 64. 3:16-21   Egypt and Edom

Amos

- 65. 1:3-5   Damascus (Syria)
- 66. 1:6-8   Philistia
- 67. 1:9-10   Tyre
- 68. 1:11-12   Edom
- 69. 1:13-15   Ammon
- 70. 2:1-3   Moab
- 71. 2:4-5   Judah
- 72. 2:6-9:15   Israel

Obadiah

- 73. 1:1-19   Edom

Jonah

- 74. 3:1-4:11   Nineveh capital of Assyria

Micah

- 75. 1:1-7:20   Samaria/Israel and Jerusalem/Judah

Nahum

- 76. 1:1-3:19   Nineveh capital of Assyria

Habakkuk

    77. 1:1-3:19   Violence of Babylon

Zephaniah

    78. 1:1-18   Whole Earth

    79. 2:1-3   Judah

    80. 2:4-7   Philistia

    81. 2:8-11   Moab and Ammon

    82. 2:12   Cush

    83. 2:13-15   Assyria

    84. 3:1-20   Jerusalem

Haggai

    85. 1:1-2:23   Judah to rebuild the Temple so God's people can Party!

Zechariah

    86. 9:1-8   Lebanon, Damascus, Tyre, Sidon and Philistia

    87. 9:9-17   Greece

    88. 10:1-12   Egypt and Assyria

    89. 11:1-3   Lebanon

    90. 12:1-14:21   Israel and Jerusalem

Malachi

    91. 1:1-4:6   Israel's broken covenants

Jesus in the New Testament

Matthew

92.	11:20-22	Chorazin and Bethsaida
93.	11:23-24	Capernaum
94.	12:38-45	Israel (Nineveh repented)

Luke

95.	10:13-14	Chorazin and Bethsaida
96.	10:15-16	Capernaum
97.	11:29-32	Israel (Nineveh repented)

98. In all Four Gospels there are a many verses against the Pharisees, Sadducees, Elders, Scribes and priests

Revelation

99.	2:18-29	Jezebel
100.	14:8	Babylon
101.	16:17-18:24	Babylon
102.	20:7-10	Devil, Cog and Magog

APPENDIX B

The Lock and Load Prophecies have been arranged according to the specific nation, its false god(s) and the signs/symptoms of that stronghold. Additional nations have been added for your study.

Please note: In order to fit the columns on the page and keep the font large enough for ease of reading and reference, the tables (beginning on the following page) have been created for you in a landscape presentation.

Nation/City	False god	Signs & Symptoms	Lock and Load Prophesies
Ammon	Molech/Milcom 1 Kings 11:5-7 & 33 2 Kings 23:10-13	Shame	Isa. 30:27-33 Jer. 29:14 & 30:3 Jer. 32:35 & 49:1-6 Ezek. 21:18-32 Ezek. 25:1-11 Amos 1:13-15 & 5:26 Zeph. 2:8-11
Moab	Chemosh Leviathan Job 41:1-34	Pride Arrogance	Isa. 2:11-18 & 10:5-19 Isa. 15:1-16:14 Isa. 25:9-12 & 27:1 Jer. 48:1-47 Ezek. 25:8-11 Amos 2:1-11 Zeph. 2:8-11

APPENDIX B | 137

Nation/City	False god	Signs & Symptoms	Lock and Load Prophesies
Edom	Lilith (Vampire)	Unforgiveness	Isa. 21:11-12 & 30:15
	Qos	Perpetual hatred	Isa. 34:1-17
			Jer. 49:7-22
			Lam. 4:21-22
			Ezek. 16:57 & 23:29
			Ezek. 25:8-14 & 32:29
			Ezek. 35:1-15 & 36:1-7
			Joel 3:1-21
			Amos 1:11-12
			Obadiah 1:1-21
			Heb. 11:20
Philistia	Dagon	Sorcery	1 Sam.13:16-27
	1 Sam. 5:1-12	Songs of Magic	Isa. 2:6 & 14:28-32
	Ashtoreth		Jer. 47:1-7
	1 Sam. 31:10		Ezek. 16:27 & 57
	Beelzebub		Ezek. 25:15-17
	2 Kings 1:2		Joel 3:1-21
	Baal		Amos 1:6-8
	Judges 2:13		Zeph. 2:4-7
			Zech. 9:1-8

Nation/City	False god	Signs & Symptoms	Lock and Load Prophesies
Phoenicia/Tyre	Astarte	Sex Worship	1 Kings 5:13-32
	Baal		1 Kings 7:1-51 & 11:5
	Judges 2:11-13		1 Chron. 14:8-12 & 22:4
	Asherah		Isa. 23:1-8
	Judges 3:7		Jer. 25:22
			Ezek. 26:1-28:19
			Joel 3:1-21
			Amos 1:9-10 & 3:11
			Zech. 9:1-8,
			Matt. 11:22 & 15:21-28
			Mk. 7:24-30
			Lk. 10:14
Sidon	Ashtoreth	To destroy	Ezek. 27:8, 28:20-26, & 32:30
	1 Kings 5:6 & 11:1-33	the Covenant	Jer. 25:22, 27:3 & 47:4
	Yam		Joel 3:1-21
	Isa. 23:1-12-NET		Zech. 9:1-8
			1 Chron. 22:4
			Luke 4:23-30 & 10:14
			Acts 27:3

APPENDIX B | 139

Nation	False god	Signs & Symptoms	Lock and Load Prophesies
Lebanon	Astarte	Sex Worship	1 Kings 7:1-51
	Baal		Isa. 10:34
			Isa. 65:1-11
			Psa. 29:5-6 & 92:12
			Zech. 9:1-8 & 11:1-3
Greece/Javan	Zeus	Sex Trafficking	Isa.60:8-9 & 66:18-23
	Mercury	Drunkenness	Ezek. 27:13-19
	Acts 14:12 Matt. 15	Debauchery	Ezek. 38:1-39:29
	Dionysus		Dan. 8:1-27, 10:20 & 11:2-4
	2 Macc. 6:7 & 14:33		Joel 3:1-21
	3 Macc. 2:29		Amos 2:6
			Joel 3:1-21
			Zech. 9:9-17
			Psa. 48 & 72
			Mk. 7:31-37
			John 12:19-21
			Acts 11:0, 14:1, 16:6-10, 17:4-12
			Acts 18:4-17, 19:10-17 & 20:2-21
			Rom. 1:14-16; Col. 3:11

Nation/City	False god	Signs & Symptoms	Lock and Load Prophesies
Syria/Aram	Hadad	Violence	Isa. 17:1-17
Damascus	Jer. 49:27	Cruelty	Jer. 49:23-27
& Antioch	Ashima		Ezek. 7:23
	2 Kings 5:18 & 17:20-30		Dan. 11:5-35
	Asherah		Amos 1:3-5
	Isa. 17:8		Zech. 9:1-8
	Adonis		Acts 9:19
	Isa. 17:10		Acts 22:10
			Gal. 1:17
Assyria & Nineveh	Belial	Oppression	Isa. 9:4
	Molech	Cruelty	Isa. 10:1-34
	Isa. 30:33-Amp	Worthlessness	Isa. 19:23-25
	Adrammelech	Failure	Isa. 30:27-33
	Anammelech	Poverty	Isa. 37:21-38
	2 Kings 17:31	Violence	Ezek. 23:5-13
			Ezek. 32:22-23
			Jonah 1:1-4:11
			Nahum 1:1-3:19

APPENDIX B | 141

Nation/City	False god	Signs & Symptoms	Lock and Load Prophesies
			Zeph. 2:13-15
			Zech. 10:1-12
			Matt. 12:38-45
			Luke 11:29-32

Other Nations Listed in the Bible

Nation/City	False god	Signs & Symptoms	Lock and Load Prophesies
Egypt	Ra	Sorcery	Isa. 19:1-20:6
	Amon	World System	Isa. 30:6-26
	Apis	Slavery	Jer. 43:12-13
			Jer. 46:2-28
			Ezek. 13:17-23
			Ezek. 23:3-27
			Ezek. 29:1-32:32
			Dan. 11:5-35
			Joel 3:1-21
			Zech. 10:1-12

Nation/City	False god	Signs & Symptoms	Lock and Load Prophesies
Cush/Ethiopia	Amon	Confusion	Isa. 18:1-7 & 21:1-6
			Isa. 45:14
			Jer. 13:23, 38:7-13
			Jer. 39:16-18
			Ezek. 30:1-12
			Zeph. 2:12 & 3:10
			Acts 8:26-40
Arabia, Kedar, Fate & Midian		Wander Aimlessly	Isa. 21:13-17 & 42:10-13
		Chaos	Isa. 46:10-13 & 60:6-7
			Isa. 65:11
			Jer. 2:10 & 25:24
			Jer. 49:28-33
			Ezek. 27:21
Amalekites or Agagites	Hmrq	Chaos	Ex. 17:8-16
		Attack from Behind	Num.14:25-45 13:22-29, 33:40. Deut. 25:17-19
		Hopelessness	1 Sam. 14:48 & 15:2-25

APPENDIX B | 143

Nation/City	False god	Signs & Symptoms	Lock and Load Prophesies
			1 Sam. 27:8, 28:18, & 30:1-18
			2 Sam. 1:1-13, & 8:12.
			1 Chron. 4:43, 10:13 & 18:11. Psa. 83:7
			Isa. 30:1-26
			Ezek. 20:45-49.
			Esther 1:1-10:3
Jezebel	Baal	Sorcery	2 Kings 9:1-37 1
	Asherah	Seduction	1 Kings 21:1-29
	1 Kings 18:1-40	Steal our zeal	Rev. 2:18-29
Babylon	Lucifer	Sorcery	Isa. 13:1-14:23
	Isa. 14:12	Violence	Isa. 21:1-10 & 26:20-27:1
	Bel	Silences God's Roar	Isa. 46:1-47:15 & 47:5-13
	Jer. 50: & 51:44	Seduction	Isa. 48:14-20
	Marduk	Perverts God's	Jer. 25:12-14 & 28:1-16
	Isa. 46:1	Calling	Jer. 50:1-51:64
			Hab. 1:1-3:19
			Ezek. 19:9 & 21:18-27
			Mic. 4:1; Zech. 2:7 & 6:10
			Rev. 14:8 & 6:17-18:24

Nation/City	False god	Signs & Symptoms	Lock and Load Prophesies
Gog and Magog			Ezek. 38:1-39:29
			Rev. 20:7-10
Antichrist			Dan. 11:36-45
			2 Thess. 2:8-9
			1 John 2:18-22 & 4:1-4
			2 John 1:7
Elam	False salvation	Demonic Intercessors	Ezra 4:9-10
			Isa. 11:11, 21:2, & 22:6-8
			Isa. 25:25 & 66:19
			Jer. 25:25 & 49:34-39
			Ezek. 32L24-25
			Dan. 8:2
Judah/Jerusalem	Too many to list!		Isa. 22:1-14
Israel/Samaria	Mot/spirit of Death		Isa. 26:1-21
	Isa. 28:15-JB		Isa. 27:2-13, 29:1-30:5
			Isa. 31:1-33:24
			Isa. 40:1-45:25
			Isa. 48:1-66:24

APPENDIX B | 145

Nation/City	False god	Signs & Symptoms	Lock and Load Prophesies
			Ezek. 16:20-63 & 23:1-49
			Ezek. 36:1-38 & 37:1-28
			Hosea 1:1-14:9
			Joel 1:1-2:32
			Amos 2:4-9:15 & 4:1-5
			Micah 1:1-7:20
			Zeph. 2:1-3 & 3:1-20
			Haggai 1:1-2:23
			Zech. 12:1-14:21
			Mal. 1:1-4:6

New Testament	Church	What to Overcome	Prophetic Word Weapon
Revelation 2-4	Ephesus	Tested False Apostles	Jesus holds the 7 stars and
Jesus' words to	(1:1-7)	Hate the Nicolaitians	Walks among the 7 lampstands
the 7 Churches		But they left their	Repent and do the first works
		first love	Eat of the Tree of Life
			Covenant with Adam

New Testament	Church	What to Overcome	Prophetic Word Weapon
	Smyrna (1:8-11)	False Jews Synagogue of satan Suffer Tribulation	The First and the Last Was dead now Alive Remain faithful Crown of life Not harmed by second death Covenant with Noah
	Pergamum (1:12-17)	Throne of satan Followers of Balaam and Nicolaitians	Sharp, two-edged Sword Eat of hidden manna White stone with new name Covenant with Moses
	Thyatira (1:18-29)	Jezebel Secrets of satan	Eyes like fire/feet like bronze Power over the nations Rule them with an iron rod Given the Morning Star Covenant with Abraham
	Sardis (2:1-6)	Dead church Deeds incomplete Wake up	7-fold Spirit and Stars Clothed in white garments Name not erased from the Book Covenant with Palestine

APPENDIX B | 147

New Testament	Church	What to Overcome	Prophetic Word Weapon
	Philadelphia (2:7-13)	Synagogue of satan will fall at your feet Hold tight to what you have	The Holy and True One Who has the Keys of David Church of the Open Door Made a Pillar in God's Temple Never leave God's presence They will have the name of God and the city of My God and My own new Name inscribed upon them. Covenant with David
	Laodicea (2:14-22)	Lukewarm church Not hot or cold Miserable, pathetic, Poor, blind and naked	The Amen, the Faithful and True Witness, Beginning of God's Creation Buy gold, clean white garments, and eye medicine from Jesus. Those Jesus loves, He corrects and disciplines He stands at the door knocking, open the door, let Him in and fellowship with Him Sit at His right hand Covenant with Jesus

NOTE: This New Testament list is also incomplete. There are many more words of instruction and correction in the New Covenant for the Church of the First Century. Their instructions still apply to us today.

APPENDIX C

List of Bible Translations and Abbreviations

Throughout this book, I have used wording from many translations, combining them for clearer understanding. I have denoted all the versions used following each reference, even though it may only have been a few words. Many people paraphrase scripture, and some may criticize my approach as trying to manipulate words or make the verses say what I want them to say to back up my concepts.

Nothing could be further from the truth. I honor God's Word. I appreciate the thought and labor that has gone into each translation—knowing that every word was painstakingly considered, compared, and thoughtfully chosen. It is this respect that drives me to be so careful in citing source material. The list below is my best effort to provide accurate copyright information and give proper credit to publishers and authors alike. I invite you to look into these resources and study them for yourself. The richness of the language of the Bible is a beautiful thing!

James M. Massa
September, 2016

- **AAT – An American Translation**
  Portions of scripture taken from *The Holy Bible in the Language of Today, AN AMERICAN TRANSLATION* are marked AAT. William F. Beck. Copyright © by William F. Beck. A.J. Holman Company. Philadelphia, PA,

- **AB – Aramaic Bible**
  Portions of scripture taken from the *Aramaic Bible* are marked AB. Vic Alexander. Burbank, CA. Retrieved at: http://www.v-a.com/bible.

- **AEB – (2001 Translation) An American English Bible**
  Portions of scripture taken from *An American English Bible* are marked AEB. Jim Wheeler, Editor. Retrieved at: http://www.2001translation.com.

- **AMP – Amplifed® Bible**
  Portions of scripture taken from the *Amplifed® Bible* are marked AMP. Copyright © 1954, 1958, 1962, 1964, 1965, 1987 by The Lockman Foundation. Used by permission. www.lockman.org

- **ARTB – Ancient Roots Translinear Bible**
  Portions of scripture taken from the *Ancient Roots Translinear Bible* are marked ARTB. A. Francis Werner. Copyright © 2005, 2006. Used by permission of the author."

- **ASV – American Standard Version**
  Portions of scripture taken from the *American Standard Version* are marked ASV. This Bible is in the public domain. © 1901.

- **BBE – The Bible in Basic English**
  Portions of scripture taken from the *The Bible in Basic English* are marked BBE. C. K. Ogden. New York, NY: Cambridge University Press, (© date unavailable).

APPENDIX C | 151

- **CAB – The Complete Apostles Bible**
  Portions of scripture taken from *The Complete Apostles Bible* are marked CAB. Paul W. Esposito; *The Complete Apostles' Bible*. Paul W. Esposito, ed. Bloomington, IL: Authorhouse, © 2005.

- **CCB – Christian Community Bible 2nd Edition**
  Portions of scripture taken from the *Christian Community Bible 2nd Edition* are marked CCB. Bernardo Hurault © 1988; *Christian Community Bible, 2nd Edition*. Bernardo Hurault. Madrid, Spain: San Pablo Internacional and Editorial Verbo Divino,

- **CEB – Common English Bible**
  Portions of scripture taken from the *Common English Bible* are marked CEB. Copyright © 2011 by Common English Bible. Retrieved from http://www.commonenglishbible.com.

- **CEV – *Contemporary English Version***
  Portions of scripture taken from the *Contemporary English Bible* are marked CEV. Copyright © 1995 by American Bible Society; *The Promise: Contemporary English Version*. Nashville, TN: Thomas Nelson Publishers, 1995.

- **CJB – Complete Jewish Bible**
  Portions of scripture taken from the *Complete Jewish Bible* are marked CEB. Copyright © 1998 by David H. Stern. Jewish New Testament Publications, Inc. Clarksville, MD.

- **CV – Confraternity Version of The Old Testament**
  Portions of scripture taken from the *Confraternity of Christian Doctrine Translation; The Old Testament of the Holy Bible: Confraternity Version* are marked CV. Copyright © 1964 by Joseph A. Grispino. New York, NY: Guild Press.

- **CW – The Clear Word**
  Portions of scripture taken from *The Clear Word* are marked CW. Paraphrased by Jack J. Blanco; Copyright © 2003 by Jack J. Blanco All rights reserved. Hagerstown, MD.

- **Dar – Darby Translation**
  Portions of scripture taken from the *Darby Translation* are marked Dar. This Bible is in the public domain.

- **DRB – Douay-Rheims 1899 American Edition.**
  Portions of scripture taken from the *Douay-Rheims* © *1899 American Edition* are marked DRB. This Bible is in the public domain.

- **ERV – Holy Bible: Easy-to-Read Version™**
  Portions of scripture taken from the *Holy Bible: Easy to Read Version*™ are marked ERV. Copyright © 2006 by World Bible Translation Center, Inc. and used by permission.

- **ESV – English Standard Version**
  Portions of scripture taken from the *English Standard Version* are marked ESV. Copyright © 2001 by Crossway Bibles, a division of Good News Publishers. Used by permission. All rights reserved.

- **EXB – The Expanded Bible**
  Portions of scripture taken from *The Expanded Bible* are marked EXB. Copyright © 2011 by Thomas Nelson, Inc. Used by permission. All rights reserved.

- **GNB – Good News Bible**
  (also known as Today's English Version – TEV)
  Portions of scripture taken from the *Good News Bible: The Bible in Today's English Version* are marked GNB. Copyright © 1976 by the American Bible Society. New York, NY.

- **GNT – Good News Translation**
  Portions of scripture taken from the *Good News Translation, Second Edition, Today's English Version* are marked GNT. Copyright © 1992 by American Bible Society. Used by permission. All rights reserved.

- **GOD'S WORD – God's Word Translation**
  Portions of scripture taken from *God's Word Translation* are marked GOD'S WORD. GOD'S WORD is a copyrighted work of God's Word to the Nations Bible Society. Quotations are used by permission. Copyright © 1995 by God's Word to the Nations. All rights reserved.

- **HCSB – Holman Cristian Standard Bible**
  Portions of scripture taken from the *Holman Christian Standard Bible* are marked HCSB. Copyright © 1999, 2000, 2002, 2003 by Holman Bible Publishers. All rights reserved.

- **HNV – Hebrew Names Version**
  (also known as World English Bible – WEB)
  Portions of scripture taken from the *Hebrew Names Version* are marked HNV. This Bible is in the public domain.

- **ISR – The Scriptures**
  Portions of scripture taken from *The Scriptures* are marked ISR. Copyright © 2010 by Institute for Scriptural Research. South Africa. All rights reserved.

- **ISV – International Standard Version**
  Portions of scripture taken from the *International Standard Version* are marked ISV. Copyright © 1995-2014 by ISV Foundation. All Rights Reserved Internationally. Used by permission of Davidson Press, LLC.

- **JB – The Jerusalem Bible**
  Portions of scripture taken from *The Jerusalem Bible* are marked JB. The Jerusalem Bible. Alexander Jones, General Editor. Copyright © 1966 by Darton, Longmann & Todd, Ltd. and Doubleday & Company, Inc. Garden City, NY. All rights rights reserved.

- **JUB – Jubilee Bible**
  Portions of scripture taken from the *Jubilee Bible* are marked JUB. The Jubilee Bible © 2000, 2000, 2001, 2010 by LIFE SENTENCE Publishing. All rights reserved.

- **KJV – King James Version**
  Portions of scripture taken from the *King James Version* are marked KJV. Originally published in 1611, this Bible is in the public domain.

- **Knox – Knox Bible: The Holy Bible, A Translation from the Latin Vulgate in the light of the Hebrew and Greek Originals**
  Portions of scripture taken from the *Knox Bible* are marked Knox. Monsignor Ronald Knox. Copyright © 1961 by Burns and Oates, London, England. Copyright pertains to all countries which are signatories to the Berne Convention.

- **LEB – Lexham® English Bible**
  Portions of scripture taken from the *Lexham English Bible* are marked LEB. Copyright © 2012 by Logos Bible Software. Lexham is a registered trademark of Logos Bible Software.

- **MLB – The Modern Language Bible**
  Portions of scripture taken from *The Modern Language Bible* iare marked MLB. The New Berkeley Version. Gerrit Verkuyl, Editor-in-Chief. Copyright © 1945, 1959, 1969, 1971 by Zondervan Publishing House. Grand Rapids, MI.

- **MNT – Montgomery New Testament**
  Portions of scripture taken from the *Montgomery New Testament, The New Testament in Modern English Translated* are marked MNT. Helen Barrett Montgomery. © 1988 by Holman Bible Publishers, Nashville.

- **Mof – A New Translation of the Bible**
  Portions of scripture taken from *A New Translation of the Bible* are marked Mof. James A. Moffatt, Editor. Copyright © 1972 Harper & Row Publishers New York, NY.

- **MRB – The Modern Reader's Bible**
  Portions of scripture taken from *The Modern Reader's Bible* are marked MRB. Richard G. Moulton Copyright © 1895, 1896, 1897, 1898, 1899, 1907, 1923, 924, 1925, 1926, 1927, and 1935. by Macmillan Co. New York, NY.

- **MSG – The Message**
  Portions of scripture taken from the *THE MESSAGE* are marked MSG. by Eugene H. Peterson. Copyright © 1993, 1994, 1995, 1996, 2000, 2001, 2002. Used by permission of NavPress Publishing Group.

- **NAB – New American Bible**
  Portions of scripture taken from the *New American Bible* are marked NAB. The text of the *New American Bible* is reproduced by license of Confraternity of Christian Doctrine, Washington, D.C.; the owner of said Bible. Copyright © 1970 by P.J. Kenedy & Sons, New York, NY. All rights reserved.

- **NASB – New American Standard Bible**
  Portions of scripture taken from the *New American Standard Bible* are marked NASB. Copyright © 1960, 1962, 1963, 1968, 1971, 1972, 1973, 1975, 1977, 1995 by The Lockman Foundation. Used by permission.

- **NCV – New Century Version**
  Portions of scripture taken from the *The Holy Bible, New Century Version*® are marked NCV. Copyright © 1987, 1988, 1991, by Word Publishing, Dallas, TX. Used by permission.

- **NEB – The New English Bible**
  Portions of scripture taken from *The New English Bible* are marked NEB. Donald Ebor, Chairman. Copyright © 1974 by Cambridge University Press. Oxford, England.

- **NET – New English Translation**
  Portions of scripture taken from the *New English Translation (The NET Bible*®*)* are designated NET. Scripture quoted by permission. Copyright © 1996-2006 by Biblical Studies Press. All rights reserved.

- **NETS – New English Translation of the Septuagint**
  Portions of scripture taken from the *New English Translation of the Septuagint* are marked NETS. Pietersma & Wright. Copyright © 2007 by the International Organization for Septuagint and Cognate Studies, Inc. Used by permission of Oxford University Press. All rights reserved.

- **NIRV – New International Reader's Version**
  Portions of scripture taken from the *New International Reader's Version*® are marked NIRV. Copyright © 1995, 1996, 1998 by International Bible Society. Used by permission of Zondervan. All rights reserved.

- **NIV – New International Version**
  Portions of scripture taken from the *Holy Bible, New International Version*®, NIV® are marked NIV. Copyright © 1973, 1978, 1984 by the International Bible Society. Used by permission of Zondervan Publishing House. All rights reserved. The "NIV" and "New International Version" are trademarks registered

in the United States Patent and Trademark Office by the International Bible Society. Use of either trademark requires the permission of the International Bible Society.

- **NIVUK – New International Version: UK**
  Portions of scripture taken from the *Holy Bible, New International Version® Anglicized, NIV®* are marked NIVUK. Copyright © 1979, 1984, 2011 by Biblica, Inc.® Used by permission. All rights reserved worldwide.

- **NJB – New Jerusalem Bible**
  Portions of scripture taken from the *New Jerusalem Bible* are marked NJB. Copyright © 1999 by Doubleday, a division of Random House, Inc., and Darton, Longman & Todd Ltd. New York, NY.

- **NKJV – New King James Version**
  Portions of scripture taken from the *New King James Version* are marked NKJV. Copyright © 1979, 1980, 1982 by Thomas Nelson, Inc. Used by permission. All rights reserved.

- **NLT – New Living Translation**
  Portions of scripture taken from *The Holy Bible, New Living Translation* are marked NLT. Copyright © 1996. Used by permission by Tyndale House Publishers, Inc., Wheaton, IL. All rights reserved.

- **NLV – New Life Version**
  Portions of scripture taken from the *Holy Bible, New Life Version* are marked NLV. Copyright © 1969 – 2003 by Christian Literature International, Canby, OR. Used by permission.

- **Noli – The New Testament of our Lord and Savior Jesus Christ**
  Portions of scripture taken from *The New Testament of our Lord and Savior Jesus Christ by* Metropolitan Fan S. Noli are marked Noli. Copyright © 1961 Albanian Orthodox Church in America, Boston. Website at http://www.albanianorthodox.com/tekste/liturgjike/Noli_1961.pdf.

- **NRSV – New Revised Standard Version**
  Portions of scripture taken from the *New Revised Version Bible* are marked NRSV. Copyright © 1989 the Division of Christian Education of the National Council of the Churches of Christ in the United States of America. Used by permission. All rights reserved.

- **NTPE – The New Testament: A New Translation in Plain English**
  Portions of scripture taken from *The New Testament: A New Translation in Plain English* are marked NTPE. Charles Kingsley Williams. Copyright © 1952 by Longman, Green & Co, University Press, Cambridge.

- **OJB – Orthodox Jewish Bible**
  Portions of scripture taken from the *Orthodox Jewish Bible* are marked OJB. Copyright © 2002, 2003, 2008, 2010 by Artists for Israel International. All rights reserved.

- **Phi – Four Prophets Amos, Hosea, First Isaiah, Micah: A Modern Translation from the Hebrew**
  Portions of scripture taken from the *Four Prophets Amos, Hosea, First Isaiah: Micah: A Modern Translation from Hebrew* are marked Phi. J. B. Phillips. Copyright © 1963 by The Macmillan Company. New York, NY.

APPENDIX C

- **PHILLIPS – J. B. Phillips New Testament**
  Portions of Scripture taken from the *J.B. Phillips New Testament, The New Testament in Mondern English* are marked PHILLIPS. Copyright © 1960, 1972 J.B. Phillips. Administered by The Archbishop's Council of the Church of Englad. Used by permission.

- **REB – The Revised English Bible**
  Portions of scripture taken from *The Revised English Bible* are marked REB. Copyright © 1989. Revision of the New English Bible Oxford, Cambridge Press.

- **Rhm – The Emphasized Bible**
  Portions of scripture taken from *The Emphasized Bible* are marked Rhm. Joseph Bryant Rotherham. Copyright © 1959, 1994 by Kregel Publications. Grand Rapids, MI.

- **RSV – Revised Standard Version**
  Portions of scripture taken from the *Revised Standard Version* are marked RSV. Copyright © 1946, 1952, and 1971 by the Division of Christian Education of the National Council of the Churches of Christ in the United States of America. Used by permission All rights reserved;

- **Sept – The Holy Bible from the Greek (Septuagint)**
  Portions of scripture taken from *The Holy Bible from the Greek (Septuagint)* are marked Sept. Charles Thompson, J. Aitken, PA. Retrieved at: http://thetencommandmentsministry.us/ministry/charlesthompson_thompson.

- **TLB – The Living Bible**
  Portions of scripture taken from *The Living Bible* are marked TLB. Kenneth N. Taylor. Copyright © 1971. Used by permission of Tyndale House Publishers, Inc., Wheaton, IL. All rights reserved.

- **TNIV – Today's New International Version**
  Portions of scripture taken from *Today's New International Version®* are marked TNIV. Copyright © 2001, 2005 by International Bible Society®. All rights reserved.

- **tPt — The Passion Translation**
  - Scripture quotations marked tPt are taken from *The Psalms: Poetry on Fire, The Passion Translation®*, copyright © 2014. Used by permission of Broadstreet Publishing Group, LLC, Racine, Wisconsin, USA. All rights reserved.

  - Scripture quotations marked tPt are taken from *Matthew: Our Loving King, The Passion Translation®*, copyright © 2014. Used by permission of Broadstreet Publishing Group, LLC, Racine, Wisconsin, USA. All rights reserved.

  - Scripture quotations marked tPt are taken from *Mark: Miracles and Mercy, The Passion Translation®*, copyright © 2014. Used by permission of Broadstreet Publishing Group, LLC, Racine, Wisconsin, USA. All rights reserved.

  - Scripture quotations marked tPt are taken from *Luke and Acts: To the Lovers of God, The Passion Translation®*, copyright © 2014. Used by permission of Broadstreet Publishing Group, LLC, Racine, Wisconsin, USA. All rights reserved.

  - Scripture quotations marked tPt are taken from *John: Eternal Love, The Passion Translation®*, copyright © 2014. Used by permission of Broadstreet Publishing Group, LLC, Racine, Wisconsin, USA. All rights reserved.

  - Scripture quotations marked tPt are taken from *Romans: Grace and Glory, The Passion Translation®*, copyright © 2015. Used by permission of Broadstreet Publishing Group, LLC, Racine, Wisconsin, USA. All rights reserved.

APPENDIX C

- Scripture quotations marked tPt are taken from *1 & 2 Corinthians: Love and Truth, The Passion Translation®*, copyright © 2014. Used by permission of Broadstreet Publishing Group, LLC, Racine, Wisconsin, USA. All rights reserved.

- Scripture quotations marked tPt are taken from *Letters from Heaven by the Apostle Paul, The Passion Translation®*, copyright © 2014. Used by permission of Broadstreet Publishing Group, LLC, Racine, Wisconsin, USA. All rights reserved.

- Scripture quotations marked tPt are taken from *Hebrews and James: Faith Works, The Passion Translation®*, copyright © 2014. Used by permission of Broadstreet Publishing Group, LLC, Racine, Wisconsin, USA. All rights reserved.

- **Voice – The Voice Bible**
Portions of scripture taken from *The Voice™ Bible* are marked Voice. Copyright © 2012 by Thomas Nelson, Inc. Ecclesia Bible Society.

- **WEB – World English Bible**
Portions of scripture taken from the *World English Bible™* are marked WEB. This Bible is in the public domain.

- **Wey – The New Testament in Modern Speech**
Portions of scripture taken from *The New Testament in Modern Speech* are marked Wey. Copyright © 1944 by Richard Francis Weymouth. The Pilgrim Press, Boston.

- **Wuest – The New Testament an Expanded Version**
Portions of scripture taken from *The New Testament an Expanded Version* are marked Wuest. Kenneth S. Wuest. Copyright © 2012 by William B. Eerdmans Publishing Company. Grand Rapids, MI.

- **WYC – Wycliff Bible**
  Portions of scripture taken from the *Wycliff Bible* are marked WYC. Copyright © 2001 by Terence P. Noble. Retrieved at http://www.ibiblio.org.

- **YLT – Young's Literal Translation**
  Portions of scripture taken from the *Young's Literal Translation* are marked YLT. This Bible is in the public domain.

MEET THE AUTHOR

James "Mark" Massa

James M. Massa is a retired Lieutenant Colonel with thirty years in the military—a veteran of both the Vietnam War and the War on Terror. He served six years with the U.S. Marines and 24 years with the U.S. Air Force. His last five years in the Air Force (2008-2012) were spent serving as the Chief Nurse in the 118th Medical Group of the 118th Airlift Wing in Nashville, TN.

Massa's service in the Marines taught him the importance of knowing his weapons and how to fight. His service in the Air Force medical field taught him the importance of knowing how to heal those who were wounded in the fight.

This military background coupled with the Hebrew meaning of his last name (massa/burden) provoked this decades-long study—the result of which you hold in your hands. Mark passionately communicates how God's songs against His enemies are available for our warfare. He wants you to learn how to use these divine WMD's from God's arsenal.

Married to his wife, Sharon, for 34 years, together they have three sons: Mark-Aaron, Seth Josiah and Fredrick (Rick) James (married to Megan). They own a small ranch in Richardsville, KY, caring for four horses, three dogs and two cats.

James & Sharon Massa